Understanding the Science of Climate Change

Talking Points - Impacts to Western Mountains and Forests

Natural Resource Report NPS/NRPC/NRR—2009/090

Rachel Loehman
Rocky Mountain Research Station
Fire Sciences Laboratory
5775 West US Hwy 10
Missoula, MT 59808-9361

With special thanks to the US Forest Service's Rocky Mountain Research Station and contributions from (in alphabetical order): Michelle Bowie, Molly Cross, Jennifer Getchell, Louise Hose, Ben Jefka, Caroline Jezierski, Kathy Jope, Fritz Klasner, David Parsons, David Peterson, Kayla Sullivan, Kathy Tonnessen, and Leigh Welling. Layout and design: Sara Melena, Angie Richman and Katherine Stehli.

December 2009

U.S. Department of the Interior
National Park Service
Natural Resource Program Center
Fort Collins, Colorado

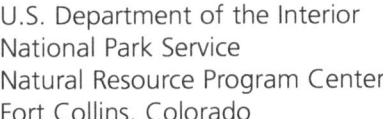

The Natural Resource Publication series addresses natural resource topics of interest and applicability to a broad readership in the National Park Service and to others in the management of natural resources, including the scientific community, the public, and the NPS conservation and environmental constituencies. Manuscripts are peer-reviewed to ensure the information is scientifically credible, technically accurate, appropriately written for the intended audience, and is designed and published in a professional manner.

Natural Resource Reports are the designated medium for disseminating high priority, current natural resource management information with managerial application. The series targets a general, diverse audience, and may contain NPS policy considerations or address sensitive issues of management applicability. Examples of the diverse array of reports published in this series include vital signs monitoring plans; monitoring protocols; "how to" resource management papers; proceedings of resource management workshops or conferences; annual reports of resource programs or divisions of the Natural Resource Program Center; resource action plans; fact sheets; and regularly-published newsletters.

Views, statements, findings, conclusions, recommendations and data in this report are solely those of the author(s) and do not necessarily reflect views and policies of the U.S. Department of the Interior, National Park Service. Mention of trade names or commercial products does not constitute endorsement or recommendation for use by the National Park Service.

This report is available from the Natural Resource Publications Management website: (http://www.nature.nps.gov/publications/NRPM)

Please cite this publication as:

Contents

I. Introduction

Purpose

Climate change presents significant risks to our nation's natural and cultural resources. Although climate change was once believed to be a future problem, there is now unequivocal scientific evidence that our planet's climate system is warming (IPCC 2007a). While many people understand that human emissions of greenhouse gases have caused recent observed climate changes, fewer are aware of the specific impacts these changes will bring. This document is part of a series of bio-regional summaries that provide key scientific findings about climate changes in and impacts to protected areas. The information is intended to provide a basic understanding of the science of climate change, known and expected impacts to resources and visitor experience, and actions that can be taken to mitigate and adapt to change. The statements may be used to communicate with managers, frame interpretive programs, and answer general questions to the public and the media. They also provide helpful information to consider in the developing sustainability strategies and long-term management plans.

Audience

The Talking Points documents are primarily intended to provide park and refuge area managers and staff with accessible, up-to-date information about climate change and climate change impacts to the resources they protect.

Organizational Structure

Following the Introduction are three major Sections of the document: a Regional section that provides information on changes to Western Mountains and Forests, a section outlining No Regrets Actions that can be taken now to mitigate and adapt to climate changes, and a general section on Global Climate Change. The Regional Section is organized around six types of changes or impacts, while the Global Section is arranged around four topics.

Regional Section

- Temperature
- The Water Cycle (including snow, ice, lake levels, sea level, and ocean acidification)
- Vegetation (plant cover, species range shifts, and phenology)
- Wildlife (aquatic, marine, and terrestrial animals, range shifts, invasive species, migration, and phenology)
- Disturbance (including range shifts, plant cover, plant pests and pathogens, fire, flooding, and erosion)
- Visitor Experience

Global Section

- Temperature and Greenhouse Gases
- Water, Snow, and Ice
- Vegetation and Wildlife
- Disturbance

Information contained in this document is derived from the published results of a range of scientific research including historical data, empirical (observed) evidence, and model projections (which may use observed or theoretical relationships). While all of the statements are informed by science, not all statements carry the same level of confidence or scientific certainty. Identifying uncertainty is an important part of science but can be a major source of confusion for decision makers and the public. In the strictest sense, all scientific results carry some level of uncertainty because the scientific method can only "prove" a hypothesis to be false. However, in a practical world, society routinely elects to make choices and select options for actions that carry an array of uncertain outcomes.

The statements in this document have been organized to help managers and their staffs differentiate among current levels of uncertainty in climate change science. In doing so, the document aims to be consistent with the language and approach taken in the Fourth Assessment on Climate Change reports by the Intergovernmental Panel on Climate Change. However, this document discriminates among only three different levels of uncertainty and does not attempt to ascribe a specific probability to any particular level. These are qualitative rather than quantitative categories and are based on the following:

- "What scientists know" are statements based on measurable data and historical records. These are statements for which scientists generally have high confidence and agreement because they are based on actual measurements and observations. Events under this category have already happened or are very likely to happen in the future.

- "What scientists think is likely" represents statements beyond simple facts; these are derived from some level of reasoning or critical thinking. They result from projected trends, well tested climate or ecosystem models, or empirically observed relationships (statistical comparisons using existing data).

- "What scientists think is possible" are statements that use a higher degree of inference or deduction than the previous categories. These are based on research about processes that are less well understood, often involving dynamic interactions among climate and complex ecosystems. However, in some cases, these statements represent potential future conditions of greatest concern, because they may carry the greatest risk to protected area resources.

II. Climate Change Impacts to Western Mountains and Forests

The Western Mountains and Forests bioregion that is discussed in this section is shown in the map to the right. A list of parks and refuges for which this analysis is most useful is included on the next page. To help the reader navigate this section, each category is designated by color-coded tabs on the outside edge of the document.

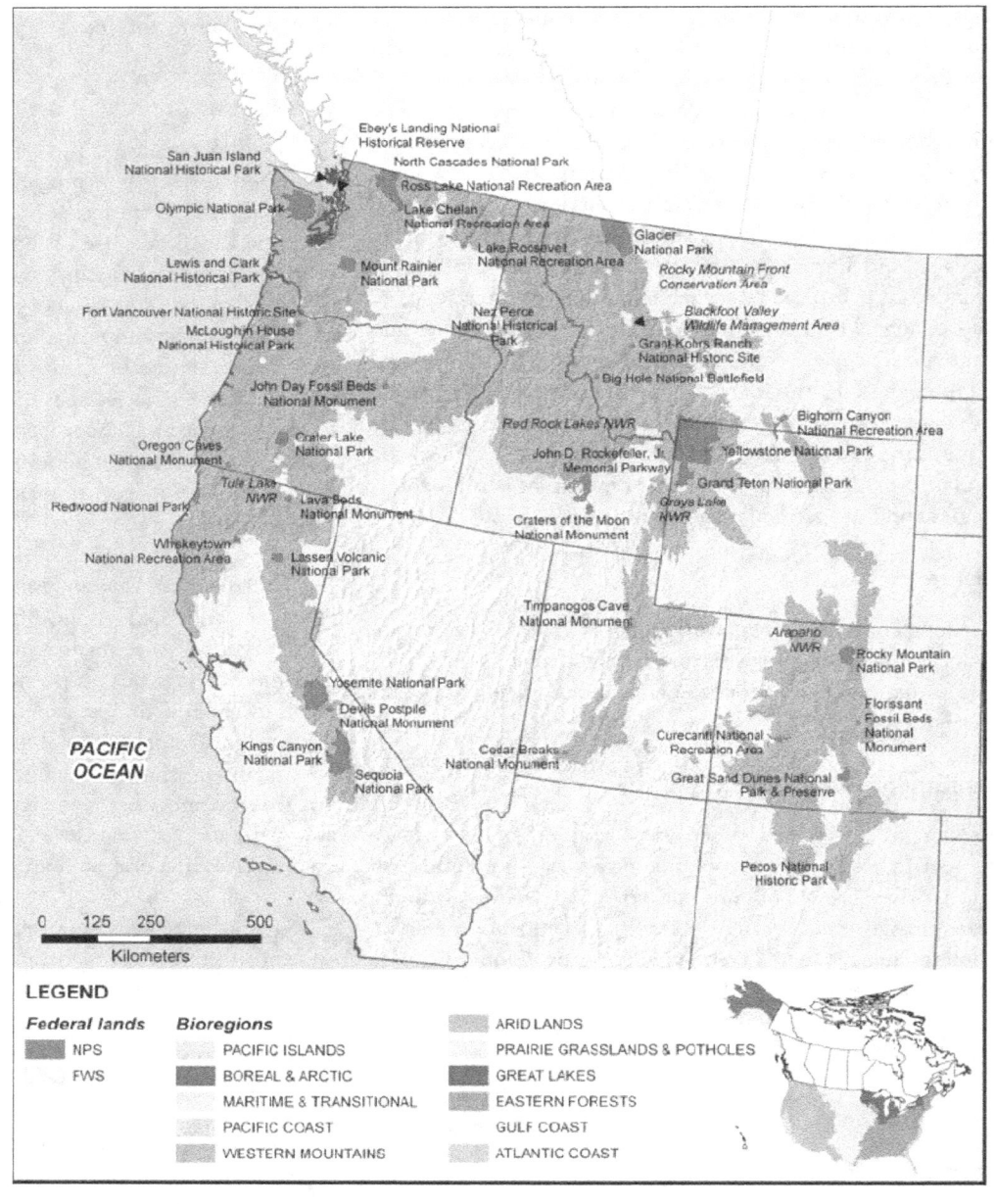

Summary

Observed climate changes in the Western Mountains and Forests bioregion include increased seasonal, annual, minimum, and maximum temperatures, altered precipitation patterns, and a shift toward earlier timing of peak runoff. These climatic changes have resulted in widespread mortality in western forests, species range shifts and changes in phenology, productivity, and distribution of species, and an increase in wildfire severity, intensity, maximum fire size, and area burned. Predicted regional changes include an increase in average temperature of around 0.3°C per decade over the next 50 years, dramatically reduced snowpack accumulation in western mountains, and commensurate reductions in runoff and natural water storage. Ecological changes likely to result from these climatic changes include continued shifts in species phenology, productivity, and distributions, species extinctions, increased frequency, size, and duration of wildfires, increased drought length and severity, and range expansion of forest pests and pathogens.

Temperature

Water Cycle

Vegetation

Wildlife

Disturbance

Visitor Experience

List of Parks and Refuges

Temperature
Water Cycle
Vegetation
Wildlife
Disturbance
Visitor Experience

U.S. National Park Service Units

- Aztec Ruins NM
- Bandelier NM
- Black Canyon of the Gunnison NP
- Big Hole NB
- Bighorn Canyon NRA
- Bryce Canyon NP
- Capulin Volcano NM
- Cedar Breaks NM
- City of Rocks NR
- Crater Lake NP
- Craters of the Moon NM
- Curecanti NRA
- Devils Postpile NM
- Devils Tower NM
- Ebey's Landing NHR
- Florissant Fossil Beds NM
- Fort Vancouver NHS
- Glacier NP
- Grand Canyon NP
- Grand Teton NP
- Grant-Kohrs Ranch NHS
- Great Basin NP
- Great Sand Dunes NP & P
- Guadalupe Mountains NP
- Jewel Cave NM
- John Day Fossil Beds NM
- John D Rockefeller Jr MP
- Kings Canyon NP
- Lake Chelan NRA
- Lake Roosevelt NRA
- Lassen Volcanic NP
- Lava Beds NM
- Lewis and Clark NHP
- Mesa Verde NP
- Mount Rainier NP
- Mount Rushmore NM
- Natural Bridges NM
- Nez Perce NHP
- North Cascades NP
- Pecos NHP
- Pinnacles NM
- Redwood NP
- Rocky Mountain NP
- Ross Lake NRA
- Olympic NP
- Oregon Caves NM
- San Juan Island NHP
- Santa Monica Mountains NRA
- Sequoia NP
- Timpanogos Cave NM
- Walnut Canyon NM
- Whiskeytown-Shasta-Trinity NRA
- Wind Cave NP
- Yellowstone NP
- Yosemite NP
- Zion NP

U.S. Fish & Wildlife Service Units

- Ankeny NWR
- Baskett Slough NWR
- Bear Valley NWR
- Benton Lake NWR
- Blackfoot Valley WMA
- Blue Ridge NWR
- Blue Ridge NWR
- Butte Sink WMA
- Camas NWR
- Clear Lake NWR
- Cold Springs NWR
- Columbia NWR
- Colusa NWR
- Conboy Lake NWR
- Deer Flat NWR
- Delevan NWR
- Dungeness NWR
- Franz Lake NWR
- Grasslands WMA
- Hart Mountain NWR
- Julia Butler Hansen NWR
- Kern NWR
- Klamath Marsh NWR
- Kootenai NWR
- Lee Metcalf NWR
- Little Pend Oreille NWR
- Lost Trail NWR
- Lower Klamath NWR
- Malheur NWR
- McKay Creek NWR
- McNary NWR
- Merced NWR
- Modoc NWR
- National Bison Range NWR
- Nine-Pipe NWR
- Nisqually NWR
- North Central Valley WMA
- Pablo NWR
- Pierce NWR
- Pixley NWR
- Protection Island NWR
- Red Rock Lakes NWR
- Ridgefield NWR
- Rocky Mountain Front Conservation Area
- Sacramento NWR
- Sacramento River NWR
- San Juan Islands NWR
- San Luis NWR
- Steigerwald Lake NWR
- Stone Lakes NWR
- Sutter NWR
- Swan River NWR
- Toppenish NWR
- Tualatin River NWR
- Tule Lake NWR
- Turnbull NWR
- Umatilla NWR
- Upper Klamath NWR
- William L. Finley NWR
- Willow Creek-Lurline WMA

Acronym	Unit Type
MP	Memorial Parkway
NB	National Battlefield
NHP	National Historic Park
NHR	National Historical Reserve
NHS	National Historic Site
NM	National Monument
NP	National Park
NR	National Reserve
NRA	National Recreation Area
NWR	National Wildlife Refuge
WMA	Wildlife Management Area

A. TEMPERATURE

What scientists know....

- Winter and spring temperatures increased in western North America during the twentieth century (Mote et al. 2005). The rate of change varies with location, but the central tendency is a warming of 1°C per century from 1916 to 2003 (Hamlet et al. 2007).

- The rate of temperature increase from 1947 to 2003 is roughly double that of the period from 1916 to 2003, largely attributable to the fact that much of the observed warming occurred from 1975 to the present. The largest temperature trends occurred in January-March (Hamlet and Lettenmaier 2007).

- Regionally averaged spring and summer temperatures for 1987 to 2003 were 0.87°C higher than those for 1970 to 1986, and spring and summer temperatures for 1987 to 2003 were the warmest since the beginning of the record in 1895 (Westerling et al. 2006).

- Air temperatures have increased 1.1–1.4°C since the early 1990s in the Loch Vale Watershed of Rocky Mountain National Park, although this is mostly a summer phenomenon and has not influenced winter snow dynamics (Clow et al. 2003).

Prehistoric granaries and the Colorado River in Marble Canyon, Grand Canyon National Park; NPS photo.

- In Colorado statewide temperatures have increased about 1.1°C over 30 years, with the greatest increase in the North Central Mountains and the least in southwestern Colorado, including the San Juan Mountains (Ray et al. 2008).

- Observational evidence shows that spring temperatures over western North America have undergone significant warming over the past half century, while autumn temperatures have shown relatively little change; however, recent research suggests that after accounting for seasonally opposite effects of atmospheric circulation, similar warming trends of around +0.2°C/decade exist for both seasons (Abatzoglou and Redmond 2007).

What scientists think is likely....

- Extreme cold temperatures are projected to increase faster than extreme warm temperatures during the next century (Kharin et al. 2007).

- All natural ecosystems of California are likely to be affected by changes in temperature and precipitation, including altered structure, composition, and productivity of vegetation communities, more frequent and intense wildfires, nonnative species invasions, and a significant rise in the number of threatened and endangered species (Lenihan et al. 2003).

- The average warming rate in the Pacific Northwest during the next ~50 years is expected to be in the range 0.1-0.6°C per decade, with a best estimate of 0.3°C per decade. For comparison, observed warming in the second half of the 20th century was approximately 0.2°C per decade (Mote et al. 2008b).

What scientists think is possible....

- Climate model simulations for the Columbia, Sacramento/San Joaquin, and Colorado River basins over the first half of the 21st century indicate a general large-scale warming of 1–2°C as compared to present (Barnett et al. 2004).

Temperature

Water Cycle

Vegetation

Wildlife

Disturbance

Visitor Experience

Repeat photography of Grinnell Glacier, Glacier National Park, showing the recession of the glacier from left to right in 1938, 1981, 1998, 2009; NPS & USGS photos.

- Regional climate models indicate that on average California may experience substantially warmer and wetter winters, somewhat warmer summers, and an enhanced El Niño Southern Oscillation (ENSO) during the 21st century (Lenihan et al. 2003).

- Regional climate projections for the northwestern United States for the late 21st century include increased frequency of extreme hot events and decreased frequency of extreme cold events, and decreased severity of cold events (Diffenbaugh et al. 2005).

B. THE WATER CYCLE

What scientists know....

- Between 1950 and 1999 there was a shift in the character of mountain precipitation, with more winter precipitation falling as rain instead of snow, earlier snow melt, and associated changes in river flow that include relative increases in the spring and relative decreases in the summer months (Mote et al. 2005, Barnett et al. 2008).

- The well-documented shift toward earlier peak runoff in the western United States in recent decades has been attributed to more precipitation falling as rain rather than snow and earlier snowmelt (Knowles et al. 2006).

- Historic patterns suggest that to date global warming has played a relatively minor role in determining cool season precipitation trends in the western United States. For example, trends in precipitation across the region have been generally upward since the early part of the century (owing primarily to large-scale drought in the early part of the record) but are opposite in sign for the Pacific Northwest and the Colorado River basin in the last half century (Hamlet and Lettenmaier 2007).

- Much of the mountainous west has experienced overall declines in spring snowpack since the mid-20th century, despite increases in winter precipitation in many places. The largest reductions have occurred where winter temperatures are mild, especially in the Cascade Mountains (where estimates of April 1 snow water equivalent indicate a 15–35% decline from mid-century to 2006) and in northern California. In most mountain ranges, there has been little change in snowpack at the highest elevations but major declines at lower elevation snow lines (Mote et al. 2005, Field et al. 2007, Mote et al. 2008a).

- Snowmelt contributes 75% of all water in streams throughout the west, and acts as a water storage reservoir. Warmer wintertime temperatures and earlier melt dates will deplete this virtual reservoir, leaving much less available water for natural systems and human uses (Service 2004).

- Mountain glaciers and snow cover have declined measurably in both hemispheres (IPCC 2007a). Since 1958, North Cascades National Park, which contains over half of the glaciers in the continental United States, has experienced a 7% reduction in glacial area and a reduced mass in 80% of the park's glaciers. In 1993 the largest glaciers in Glacier National Park were measured at 72% of their 1850 areal extent and many small glaciers had vanished. The rate of glacial melting suggests that the park's remnant glaciers will be gone in the next 25 to 30 years (Hall and Fagre 2003, Burkett et al. 2005).

- Increased precipitation variability and systematic warming associated with late 20th century climate has increased flood risks in rain-dominant basins and in many near coastal areas in Washington, Oregon, and California (Hamlet and Lettenmaier 2007).

- Recent analysis suggests that the majority of the low-frequency changes in the hydrological cycle (river flow, temperature, and snow pack) observed in the western United States from 1950 to 1999 are due to human caused climate changes from greenhouse gases and aerosols, based on differences between observed and expected trends (Barnett et al. 2008).

What scientists think is likely....

- The projected large-scale warming of 1-2°C over present-day temperatures will significantly impact water resources, including a large reduction in the volume and persistence of mountain snowpacks, and a commensurate reduction in natural water storage. Current demands on water resources in many parts of the West will not be met under plausible future climate conditions, including water supplies for natural and anthropogenic systems (Barnett et al. 2004, Knowles et al. 2006).

- Warming in the western states is expected to increase the fraction of precipitation that falls as rain rather than snow and hasten the onset of snowmelt once snowpacks have formed. Snow deposition is sensitive to wintertime (November-March) warming trends, whereas snowmelt is sensitive to changes in springtime temperatures (Knowles et al. 2006).

- Reduced snowpack and earlier runoff will mean less available water for summer irrigation needs, higher water temperatures, and increased conflict between agricultural users and those whose princi-

pal concern is sustaining fish populations. These effects will be especially profound in smaller, snowmelt-driven rivers such as the Yakima River in Washington State (Barnett et al. 2004)

- Regional warming may reduce western snowpacks by up to 60% over the next 50 years in regions such as the Cascade Mountains of Oregon and Washington. Summertime streamflows are expected to decrease in response by 20 to 50% in these areas (Service 2004).

- Changes in flood risk are likely to result in substantial changes in sediment transport and channel formation processes, and are also likely to affect ecological processes that are sensitive to changes in the probability distributions of high flow events such as habitat stability, biodiversity, and trophic structure (Konrad and Booth 2005, Hamlet and Lettenmaier 2007).

- Precipitation events that are currently considered extreme (20-year return interval) are expected to occur roughly twice as often as they currently do, consistent with general increases in rainstorm intensity (Kharin et al. 2007).

- The decline of glacial ice may be linked to increases in mean summer temperature and/or a reduction in the winter snowpack that forms and maintains glaciers (Hall and Fagre 2003).

What scientists think is possible....

- Potential hydrologic and ecological responses to earlier snowmelt modeled for the Loch Vale Watershed at Rocky Mountain National Park showed 50% reductions in snowpack and 4-5 week earlier increases in soil moisture and runoff (compared to mean onset of spring conditions from 1984 to 1998) with a 4°C temperature increase and doubling of atmospheric of CO_2 (Baron et al. 2000).

- Large- and small-scale models are consistent in their predictions for future hydrologic patterns in California; these include declines in summer low streamflows (i.e. more extremely low flows in summer) and increases in winter stream flows (i.e. more

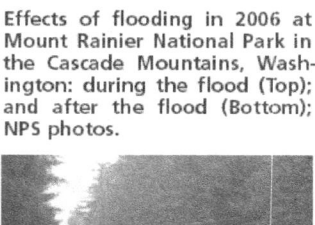

Effects of flooding in 2006 at Mount Rainier National Park in the Cascade Mountains, Washington: during the flood (Top); and after the flood (Bottom); NPS photos.

Temperature

Water Cycle

Vegetation

Wildlife

Disturbance

Visitor Experience

Temperature

Water Cycle

Vegetation

Wildlife

Disturbance

Visitor Experience

Hidden Meadow Camp at North Cascades National Park is losing ground as trees encroach into areas where they were previously unable to survive; NPS photo.

winter flooding), and a shift of runoff peaks to earlier in the year (Dettinger et al. 2004, Maurer and Duffy 2005).

- The greatest reduction in snowpack volume in the Sierra Nevada region of California is expected to occur in the elevation range of 1,300-2,700 meters. Models predict that warmer storms and earlier snowmelt will cause April snow accumulation to drop to 95% of its present levels by 2030 and 48% by 2090; these changes will result in lower spring-summer streamflows, increased salinity, and changes in species habitat in the San Francisco Estuary (the third largest estuary in the U.S.) (Knowles and Cayan 2004).

- Projected precipitation changes in the Pacific Northwest are unlikely to be distinguishable from natural variability until late in the 21st century. Most projections show winter precipitation increasing and summer precipitation decreasing and an increase in intense precipitation (Mote et al. 2008b).

C. VEGETATION

What scientists know....

- Climate has demonstrably affected terrestrial ecosystems through changes in the seasonal timing of life-cycle events (phenology), plant-growth responses (primary production), and biogeographic distribu-

tion (Parmesan 2006, Field et al. 2007). Statistically significant shifts in Northern Hemisphere vegetation phenology, productivity, and distribution have been observed and are attributed to 20th century climate changes (Walther et al. 2002, Parmesan and Yohe 2003, Root et al. 2003, Parmesan 2006).

- Growth of subalpine tree species in the Pacific Northwest is strongly influenced by climate factors including snowpack duration, summer moisture stress, and growing season length. Observed effects of climate changes in the region include displacement of subalpine meadows by tree species, infilling of previously open areas such as avalanche paths, and tree line changes (Fagre et al. 2003).

- The vegetation growing season, as defined by continuous frost-free air temperatures, has increased by on average about two days/decade since 1948 in the conterminous United States, with the largest changes occurring in the West (Ryan et al. 2008).

- Increases in minimum monthly temperature and multidecadal variability in minimum temperature and precipitation are linked to increased annual branch growth of krummholz whitebark pine, invasion by whitebark pine and western white pine into formerly persistent snowfields, timing of vertical branch emergence in krummholz whitebark pine, and invasion by lodgepole pine into subalpine meadows in upper elevation forests of the central Sierra Nevada, California (Millar et al. 2004).

- Widespread mortality events during the 20th century in forests of the West have led to conditions outside ranges of variability documented in past centuries in western North America. (CIRMOUNT 2006).

- The recent drought centered on 2000–2004 caused extensive forest dieback in the West, including 1.5 million hectares of piñon pine and 1.0 million hectares of ponderosa pine on the Colorado Plateau. Bark beetles were frequently the ultimate cause of death in dense and climate-stressed forests of this region (CIRMOUNT 2006).

- Forests in the western United States sequester 20 to 40% of U.S. carbon emissions from fossil fuels, an amount equal to about one-half of the carbon absorbed by terrestrial ecosystems in the conterminous U.S. (Pacala et al. 2001, Westerling et al. 2006, Brown 2008). Changes in forest productivity, structure, and composition will result in changes in the rate of carbon sequestration and amount of carbon stored as biomass.

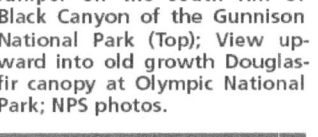

Juniper on the south rim of Black Canyon of the Gunnison National Park (Top); View upward into old growth Douglas-fir canopy at Olympic National Park; NPS photos.

- Some aquatic and terrestrial plant and microbial communities are significantly altered by nitrogen deposition, either from low level atmospheric deposition or "hotspot" deposition downwind of metropolitan areas or agricultural operations. Observed vegetation responses include increased plant productivity, biotic community changes, and deleterious effects on sensitive organisms including lichens and phytoplankton (Fenn et al. 2003).

What scientists think is likely....

- Vegetation response to changing climate will depend on the factors that limit productivity at a particular site; for example, changes in growing season length may affect annual productivity, and increased nitrogen and CO_2 inputs strongly influence forest productivity if other factors (water, temperature, radiation) are less limiting (Ryan et al. 2008).

- Forest growth is expected to decrease in regions where increased temperature coincides with decreased precipitation (western Alaska, Interior West, Southwest) (Ryan et al. 2008).

- Rising CO_2 will very likely increase photosynthesis for forests, but the increased photosynthesis will likely only increase wood production in young forests on fertile soils. Where nutrients are not limiting, rising CO_2 increases photosynthesis and wood production, but on infertile soils the extra carbon from increased photosynthesis will be quickly respired. The response of older forests to CO_2 is uncertain, but possibly will be lower than the average of the studied younger forests (Ryan et al. 2008).

- For California, models indicate a shift in dominance from needle-leaved toward broad-leaved trees, along with increases in vegetation productivity, especially in the relatively cool and mesic (moderately moist habitat, such as temperate hardwood) regions of the state (Lenihan et al. 2003).

What scientists think is possible....

- Future climate change scenarios for California predict a decline in alpine/subalpine forest cover, increases in the productivity of evergreen hardwoods and the subsequent displacement of evergreen conifer forest by mixed evergreen forest, and expansion of grasslands (Lenihan et al. 2008).

- Warmer winter temperatures may reduce the competitiveness of Douglas-fir seedlings by not providing a sufficient period of winter cold temperatures to meet the species' chilling requirements; furthermore, the distribution of Douglas-fir may decline if fire frequencies exceed 1 fire per 20 years (Whitlock et al. 2003).

- Dramatic changes in forested lands within the western U.S are expected to occur with climate shifts; these include severe contraction and northward displacement of alpine habitats, subalpine spruce-fir forests, and aspen; fragmentation and disjunction of species' ranges; and possible

Temperature

Water Cycle

Vegetation

Wildlife

Disturbance

Visitor Experience

expansion of forests into current grass- and shrublands (ISAB 2007).

• Douglas fir, Pacific yew and red alder are predicted to shift in range from west of to east of the Cascades, and the potential habitats of dominant rainforest conifers (e.g., western hemlock, western red cedar) are expected to decrease west of the Cascades but expand into mountain ranges of the interior West. In contrast, Ponderosa pine, which is tolerant of relative warm and dry climate, is predicted to expand its range significantly and to occur west of the Cascades (ISAB 2007).

D. WILDLIFE

What scientists know....

• A consistent temperature-related shift has been observed across a broad range of plant and animal species (80% of species from 143 studies), including changes in species density, north- or poleward range shifts, changes in phenology, and shifts in genetic frequencies (Root et al. 2003).

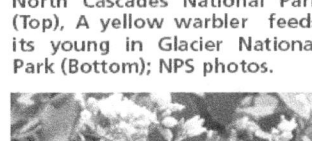

A Pale Swallowtail butterfly at North Cascades National Park (Top), A yellow warbler feeds its young in Glacier National Park (Bottom); NPS photos.

• A meta-analysis of climate change effects on range boundaries in Northern Hemisphere species of birds, butterflies, and alpine herbs shows an average shift of 6.1 kilometers per decade northward (or meters per decade upward), and a mean shift toward earlier onset of spring events (frog breeding, bird nesting, first flowering, tree

budburst, and arrival of migrant butterflies and birds) of 2.3 days per decade (Parmesan and Yohe 2003).

• Many North American wildlife species have shifted their ranges to more northerly or higher elevations. For example, the Edith's checkerspot butterfly has become locally extinct in the southern, low-elevation portion of its North American range, but has extended its range 90 kilometers north and 120 kilometers upward in elevation (Field et al. 2007).

• The northern boundary of the sachem skipper butterfly has expanded 670 kilometers from California to Washington State in the past 40 years, corresponding with areas where the winter minimum temperature has rise 3°C since 1950 (Crozier 2003). During a single year -1998, the second warmest on record - the butterfly moved 120 kilometers northward, and laboratory and field manipulations show that because winter cold extremes dictate the northern range limit, the butterfly may extend its range even further as minimum temperatures increase (Crozier 2003, 2004).

• Past physiological studies suggest that stress from increasing temperatures is the likely cause of rapid population decline and local extinctions of American pika, a cold-adapted, mountain-dwelling species that survives in isolated mountaintop islands throughout the western United States (Beever et al. 2003, NRC 2008)

• A small-mammal survey in Yosemite National Park showed substantial upward changes (~500 meters) in elevation limits for half of 28 species monitored. In addition, high-elevation species experienced range contractions and low-elevation species expanded their ranges upward (Moritz et al. 2008).

What scientists think is likely....

• American robins in the Colorado Rocky Mountains are arriving earlier in spring than in previous decades (14 days earlier in 1999 than in 1981). The interval between arrival date and the first date of bare ground has grown by 18 days, because

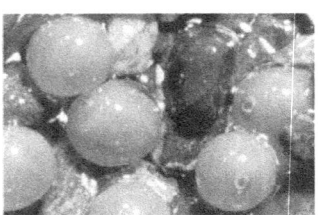

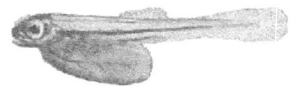

Stages of life of Chinook salmon. From top to bottom: egg, alevin, fry, smolt, ocean adult, and spawning stage; USFWS images.

the growing season onset date is occurring earlier in the year at low elevations but has remained largely unchanged at high elevation sites (Inouye et al. 2000).

- Changes in minimum and mean temperatures and amount and timing of precipitation may increase prevalence of hantavirus, plague, and West Nile virus in wildlife populations though changes in phenological development, increased rates of reproduction and survival, altered geographic distributions, and expansion of favorable habitats of disease vector, host, and reservoir species (Patz et al. 2000, Epstein 2001, Field et al. 2007).

What scientists think is possible....

- Modeling of potential future climate and vegetation scenarios indicates that potential Canada Lynx habitat may decrease significantly by 2100 because of reduced snow cover and vegetation changes. Areas that may become unsuitable for lynx include the Bridger-Teton (Wyoming), Idaho Panhandle (Idaho), Kootenai (Montana), Okanogan (Washington) and Wenatchee (Washington) National Forests; high-altitude areas in Colorado; and Yellowstone and Grand Teton National Parks (Wyoming) (Gonzalez et al. 2007).

- An analysis of potential climate change impacts on mammalian species in U.S. national parks indicates that on average about 8% of current mammalian species diversity may be lost. The greatest losses across all parks occurred in rodent species (44%), bats (22%), and carnivores (19%) (Burns et al. 2003).

- Fragmentation of large ecosystems may occur due to increased disturbance and vegetative change, disrupting existing wildlife ranges. Certain types of habitat, such as margin or edge areas, will be particularly sensitive (McCarty 2001).

- Climate change has the potential to affect most freshwater life history stages of trout and salmon. Increased frequency and severity of flood flows during winter can affect over-wintering juvenile fish and incubating eggs in the streambed. Eggs of fall and winter spawning fish, including Chinook, coho, chum, and sockeye salmon and bull trout, may suffer higher levels of mortality when exposed to increased flood flows. Higher winter water temperatures could also accelerate embryo development and cause premature emergence of fry (ISAB 2007).

- Models predict that changes in stream temperatures resulting from warming of average air temperature will result in earlier spawning for greenback cutthroat trout in the central Rocky Mountains.(Cooney et al. 2005).

- Changing vegetation cover in many park areas will affect wildlife species dependent on those habitats. Animals will eventually occupy landscapes vacated by glacial ice, and utilize new alpine lakes after ice is gone (Burkett et al. 2005).

- The synergism of rapid temperature rise and stresses such as habitat destruction may disrupt connectedness among species, lead to reformulation of species communities, and result in numerous extirpations and/or extinctions (Root et al. 2003).

- Modeled effects of elevational limits on the extinction risk of landbirds (87% of all bird species) projected a best guess of 400–550 landbird extinctions, and approximately 2150 additional species at risk of extinction, by 2100. For Western Hemisphere landbirds, intermediate extinction estimates based on climate-induced changes in actual distributions ranged from 1.3% (for 1.1°C warming) to 30.0% (for 6.4°C warming) of these species (Sekercioglu et al. 2007).

E. DISTURBANCE

What scientists know....

- The forested area burned in the western U.S. from 1987 to 2003 was more than six and a half times the area burned from 1970 to 1986. Other observed trends include more frequent large wildfires (greater than 400 ha in size), longer wildfire durations, and longer wildfire seasons. The greatest increases in wildfire activity occurred in mid-elevation Northern Rockies forests (Westerling et al. 2006).

Temperature

Water Cycle

Vegetation

Wildlife

Disturbance

Visitor Experience

- A large area (approximately 120,000 km2) of California and western Nevada experienced a notable increase in the extent of forest stand-replacing (high severity) fire and increases in mean and maximum fire size and area burned annually between 1984 and 2006. These changes in fire severity and activity are attributed to a regional increase in temperature and a long-term increase in annual precipitation (Miller et al. 2008).

The Robert Fire was one of three large fires that burned a total of 18% of Glacier National Park's vegetation cover in 2003; NPS photo.

- Climate is a strong driver of 20th century fire synchrony in the interior west of North America. In both the inland Northwest (interior Oregon, Washington, and southern British Columbia) and in the northern Rocky Mountains warm spring–summers and warm-dry summers are associated with widespread fires. Spring climate likely affected the length of the fire season via the effects of snowmelt on soil and fuel moisture, whereas summer climate influenced fuel moisture during the fire season (Heyerdahl et al. 2008, Morgan et al. 2008).

- More than 55 million acres of forested lands are currently impacted by disturbance. The largest agents of change are insects and pathogens, which cause an estimated financial loss of 3.7 billion dollars per year (Dale et al. 2001).

- A recent study in British Columbia linked an increase (at an increasing rate) in the number of mountain pine beetle infestations since 1970 with an increase in the amount of available optimal habitat. The amount of climatically optimal habitat has increased by more than 75% since around 1970, probably as the result of an average annual temperature increase of >1°C (Carroll 2006).

- Cumulative stresses in western mountain forests, triggered by climate change and fire exclusion, are affecting the resilience of forests. When periodic multiyear droughts, common in western North America, occur against a backdrop of rising temperatures and unnaturally high fuel loads, forests are vulnerable to insect and disease epidemics and severe fires. These combined effects can cause significant changes in forest composition and structure and extensive forest diebacks (CIRMOUNT 2006).

What scientists think is likely....

- Disturbance may reset and rejuvenate some ecosystems in some cases, and cause enduring change in others. For example, drought may weaken trees and make them susceptible to insect attack and death; however, fire is an integral component of many forest ecosystems and many tree

Aftermath of a 2003 forest fire at Glacier National Park (Top); In Great Basin National Park, fir engraver beetles leave trails beneath the bark of living and dead conifers (Bottom); NPS photos.

species (e.g. lodgepole pine forests) depend on fire for regeneration (Ryan et al. 2008).

- Disturbance events in the future may be larger and more common than those experienced historically, and planning for disturbances should be encouraged (Dale et al. 2001).

- Increases in frequency, size, and duration of wildfires in the western U.S. observed within the past three decades are attributed to a 78-day increase in the length of the wildfire season, increases in spring-summer temperatures of 0.87°C, and earlier spring snowmelt (Westerling et al. 2006).

- An increase in the average length and intensity of summer drought in the Northern Rockies and elsewhere in the western United States will result in an increased frequency of large wildfires and subsequent changes in forest composition. Reduced tree densities associated with large and severe wildfires may cause western forests to become a source of increased atmospheric carbon dioxide rather than a sink, even under a relatively modest temperature-increase scenario (Westerling et al. 2006).

- Over the past century, and at the scale of the whole western United States and Canada, variations and trends in temperature have been significantly correlated with numbers of large fires and areas burned.

This suggests that regional to continental warming patterns are beginning to influence fire activity at the broadest scales (CIRMOUNT 2006).

- By 2070 the length of the fire season could be increased by two to three weeks in the northern Rockies, Great Basin, and Southwest as the result of increases in summer temperature and decreases in summer humidity (Barnett et al. 2004).

- Large outbreaks of forest insects are likely influenced by observed increases in temperature because temperature controls life cycle development rates, influences synchronization of mass attacks required to overcome tree defenses, and determines winter mortality rates. Climate also affects insect populations indirectly through effects on hosts; for example, drought stress reduces the ability of a tree to mount a defense against insect attacks (Logan and Powell 2001, Ryan et al. 2008).

- Future northward range expansion attributed to warming temperatures has been predicted for mountain pine beetle, including potential invasion of jack pine, a suitable host that extends across the boreal forest of North America (Logan and Powell 2001).

- Resilience to perturbations, establishment of invasive species, and local extinction depend in large part on the degree of climatic stress that occurs directly before and after large ecological disturbances (CIRMOUNT 2006).

What scientists think is possible....

- Predicted trends in climate will reinforce the tendency toward longer fire seasons and accentuate conditions favorable to the occurrence of large, intense wildfires (e.g. increased storminess, higher fuel loads, drier conditions late in the season) (Lenihan et al. 2003, Whitlock et al. 2003, Westerling et al. 2006).

- Future climate change scenarios for California predict an increase in total area burned of 9-15% above the historical norm by 2100 (Lenihan et al. 2008).

Temperature

Water Cycle

Vegetation

Wildlife

Disturbance

Visitor Experience

Temperature

Water Cycle

Vegetation

Wildlife

Disturbance

Visitor Experience

- Simulations of potential future climate and vegetation indicate that future fire conditions in some parts of the northwestern US could be more severe than they are today. Even if summer precipitation in the region increased significantly, greater evapotranspiration as a result of higher temperatures could still lead to increased drought stress. Changes in temperature and the timing of precipitation would also affect fuel moisture levels, with drier fuels increasing the potential for fires (Whitlock et al. 2003).

- Modeling indicates that reduced net primary productivity and altered disturbance patterns may be expected in dry, east-side forest ecosystems in Montana and Washington under climatic warming conditions (Fagre and Peterson 2000).

F. VISITOR EXPERIENCE

- A visitor survey at Rocky Mountain National Park suggest that while a small number of visitors may increase park visits under a warming climate, more than 70% of respondents indicated that current opportunities for viewing conifer forests and wildflowers were important reasons for visitation to the park (Richardson and Loomis 2004).

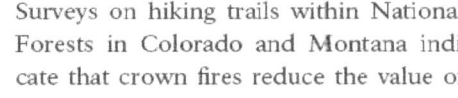

A hiker enjoys Ranger Meadow in Deadman Canyon, in the southern part of Kings Canyon National Park; NPS photo.

- Surveys on hiking trails within National Forests in Colorado and Montana indicate that crown fires reduce the value of

recreation (measured as changes in the annual value of trips taken) because of reduced aesthetic value of the landscape as perceived by respondents (Hesseln et al. 2004).

- In surveys of visitors to National Forests in Colorado, years since a non-crown fire increased the trip demand of hikers while the presence of crown fires reduced the number of mountain bike trips within the forests (Loomis et al. 2001).

- The locations of climatically ideal tourism conditions are likely to shift toward higher latitudes under projected climate change, and as a consequence spatial and temporal redistribution of tourism activities may occur. The effects of these changes will depend greatly on the flexibility demonstrated by institutions and tourists as they react to climate change (Amelung et al. 2007).

- A statistical model of monthly visitation and anticipated climate and environmental change at Waterton Lakes National Park in the Canadian Rockies projected that annual visitation would increase between 6% and 10% in the 2020s and between 10% and 36% in the 2050s as the result of an increase in the length and quality of warm-weather tourism seasons. However, 56% of respondents indicated that they would reduce or discontinue visits to the park under projected 2080s environmental conditions, which included a decline in wildlife species, disappearance of glaciers from the park, loss of rare plant species, transition from forests to grasslands, and large increase in forest fires, (Scott et al. 2007).

- Changes to the terrestrial and aquatic species compositions in parks and refuges are likely to occur as ranges shift, contract, or expand (Burns et al. 2003).

- Parks and refuges may not be able to meet their mandate of protecting current species within their boundaries, or in the case of some refuges, the species for whose habitat protection they were designed. While wildlife may be able to move northward or to higher elevations to escape

Bird watchers scan an alpine lake in Rocky Mountain National Park.; NPS photo.

some effects of climate change, federal boundaries are static (Burns et al. 2003).

- Lakeshore levels and stream depths will increasingly fluctuate, potentially making fixed docks and boat ramps unusable for much of the year. Navigational hazards and new sand bars may be exposed (Scavia et al. 2002).

- Effects of projected climate changes on human health include increased incidence of heat stress and heat stroke, respiratory distress from pollutants released during wildfires, cardio-respiratory morbidity and mortality associated with ground-level ozone, and injury and death from floods, storms, fires, and droughts (Epstein 2001, Confalonieri et al. 2007).

- Glaciers in western North America are important tourist attractions for mountain parks. Observed and projected changes in glacial extent (Hall and Fagre 2003) may have a negative effect on the number of visitors to Glacier National Park (Scott et al. 2007).

- Because of increases in fire season length and severity it is possible that visitors to mountain parks may experience more re-

strictions on their activities (e.g. campfire bans; trail and park closures) (Scott et al. 2007).

- Climate changes may favor zoonotic disease transmission to humans through altered distributions of pathogens and disease vectors, increased populations of reservoir or host species, and increased prevalence of diseases within host and reservoir populations. Diseases likely to increase in scope and/or incidence in the region include hantavirus pulmonary syndrome, plague, and West Nile virus (Epstein 2001, Confalonieri et al. 2007).

- Increasing frequency and intensity of severe storms and floods may pose threats to historic structures, roads and trails, archeological sites, administrative facilities, and other park resources and infrastructure.

- Increased summer temperatures will lead to increased utility expenditures in parks in the summer and, potentially, decreases in the winter.

- Potentially poorer visibility due to smoke from increased wildland fire activity will likely cause a negative impact on visitor experiences.

Temperature

Water Cycle

Vegetation

Wildlife

Disturbance

Visitor Experience

III. No Regrets Actions: How Individuals, Parks, Refuges, and Their Partners Can Do Their Part

Individuals, businesses, and agencies release carbon dioxide (CO_2), the principal greenhouse gas, through burning of fossil fuels for electricity, heating, transportation, food production, and other day-to-day activities. Increasing levels of atmospheric CO_2 have measurably increased global average temperatures, and are projected to cause further changes in global climate, with severe negative implications for vegetation, wildlife, oceans, water resources, and human populations. Emissions reduction – limiting production of CO_2 and other greenhouse gases - is an important step in addressing climate change. It is the responsibility of agencies and individuals to find ways to reduce greenhouse gas emissions and to educate about the causes and consequences of climate change, and ways in which we can reduce our impacts on natural resources. There are many simple actions that each of us can take to reduce our daily carbon emissions, some of which will even save money.

Agencies Can...

Improve sustainability and energy efficiency

- Use energy efficient products, such as ENERGY STAR® approved office equipment and light bulbs.

- Initiate an energy efficiency program to monitor energy use in buildings. Provide guidelines for reducing energy consumption.

- Convert to renewable energy sources such as solar or wind generated power.

- Specify "green" designs for construction of new or remodeled buildings.

- Include discussions of climate change in the park Environmental Management System.

- Establish an in-park sustainability team and develop sustainability Best Management Practices. Request and hold Climate Friendly Park workshops in cooperation with the EPA.

- Provide alternative transportation options such as employee bicycles and shuttles for within-park commuting.

- Provide hybrid electric or propane-fueled vehicles for official use, and impose fuel standards for park vehicles. Reduce the number and/or size of park vehicles and boats to maximize efficiency.

- Provide a shuttle service or another form of alternate transportation for visitor travel to and within the park.

- Provide incentives for use of alternative transportation methods.

- Use teleconferences or other forms of modern technology in place of travel to conferences and meetings.

Management Actions

- Engage and enlist collaborator support (e.g., tribes, nearby agencies, private landholders) in climate change discussions, responses, and mitigation.

- Develop strategies and identify priorities for managing uncertainty surrounding climate change effects in parks and refuges.

- Build a strong partnership-based foundation for future conservation efforts.

- Identify strategic priorities for climate change efforts when working with partners.

- Incorporate anticipated climate change impacts, such as decreases in lake levels or changes in vegetation and wildlife, into management plans.

An interpretive brochure about climate change impacts to National Parks was created in 2006 and has been distributed widely since.

Climate Change in National Parks

Park Service employees install solar panels at San Francisco Maritime National Historical Park (Top); At the National Mall, Park Service employees use clean-energy transportation to lead tours; NPS photos.

- Encourage research and scientific study in park units and refuges.

- Design long-term monitoring projects and management activities that do not rely solely on fossil fuel-based transportation and infrastructure.

- Incorporate products and services that address climate change in the development of all interpretive and management plans.

- Take inventory of the facilities/boundaries/species within your park or refuge that may benefit from climate change mitigation or adaptation activities.

- Participate in gateway community sustainability efforts.

- Recognize the value of ecosystem services that an area can provide, and manage the area to sustain these services. Conservation is more cost-effective than restoration and helps maintain ecosystem integrity.

- Provide recycling options for solid waste and trash generated within the park.

Restore damaged landscapes

- Restoration efforts are important as a means for enhancing species' ability to cope with stresses and adapt to climatic and environmental changes. Through restoration of natural areas, we can lessen climate change impacts on species and their habitats. These efforts will help preserve biodiversity, natural resources, and recreational opportunities.

- Strategically focus restoration efforts, both in terms of the types of restoration undertaken and their national, regional, and local scale and focus, to help maximize resources.

- Restore and conserve connectivity within habitats, protect and enhance instream flows for fish, and maintain and develop access corridors to climate change refugia.

- Restore natural hydrologic functions of coastal wetlands to help protect coastal areas against hurricanes and flooding.

Educate staff and the public

- Post climate change information in easily accessible locations such as on bulletin boards and websites.

- Provide training for park and refuge employees and partners on effects of climate change on resources, and on dissemination of climate change knowledge to the public.

- Support the development of region, park, or refuge-specific interpretive products on the impacts of climate change.

- Incorporate climate change research and information in interpretive and education outreach programming.

- Distribute up-to-date interpretive products (e.g., the National Park Service-wide Climate Change in National Parks brochure)

- Develop climate change presentations for local civic organizations, user and partner conferences, national meetings, etc..

- Incorporate climate change questions and answers into park-based Junior Ranger programs.

- Help visitors make the connection between reducing greenhouse gas emissions and resource stewardship.

> "Humankind has not woven the web of life. We are but one thread within it. Whatever we do to the web, we do to ourselves. All things are bound together. All things connect."
>
> —Chief Seattle

- Encourage visitors to use public or non-motorized transportation to and around parks.

- Encourage visitors to reduce their carbon footprint in their daily lives and as part of their tourism experience.

Individuals can...

- In the park or refuge park your car and walk or bike. Use shuttles where available. Recycle and use refillable water bottles. Stay on marked trails to help further ecosystem restoration efforts.

- At home, walk, carpool, bike or use public transportation. A full bus equates to 40 fewer cars on the road. When driving, use a fuel-efficient vehicle.

- Do not let cars idle - letting a car idle for just 20 seconds burns more gasoline than turning it off and on again.

- Replace incandescent bulbs in the five most frequently used light fixtures in the home with bulbs that have the ENERGY STAR® rating. If every household in the U.S. takes this one simple action we will prevent greenhouse gas emissions equivalent to the emissions from nearly 10 million cars, in addition to saving money on energy costs.

Reduce, Reuse, Recycle, Refuse

- Use products made from recycled paper, plastics and aluminum - these use 55-95% less energy than products made from scratch.

- Purchase a travel coffee mug and a reusable water bottle to reduce use of disposable products (Starbucks uses more than 1 billion paper cups a year).

- Carry reusable bags instead of using paper or plastic bags.

- Recycle drink containers, paper, newspapers, electronics, and other materials. Bring recyclables home for proper disposal when recycle bins are not available. Rather than taking old furniture and clothes to the dump, consider "recycling" them at a thrift store.

- Keep an energy efficient home. Purchase ENERGY STAR® appliances, properly insulate windows, doors and attics, and lower the thermostat in the winter and raise it in the summer (even 1-2 degrees makes a big difference). Switch to green power generated from renewable energy sources such as wind, solar, or geothermal.

- Buy local goods and services that minimize emissions associated with transportation.

- Encourage others to participate in the actions listed above.

For more information on how you can reduce carbon emissions and engage in climate-friendly activities, check out these websites:

EPA- What you can do: http://www.epa.gov/climatechange/wycd/index.html

NPS- Do Your Part! Program: http://www.nps.gov/climatefriendlyparks/doyourpart.html

US Forest Service Climate Change Program: http://www.fs.fed.us/climatechange/

United States Global Change Research Program: http://www.globalchange.gov/

U.S. Fish and Wildlife Service Climate change: http://www.fws.gov/home/climatechange/

The Climate Friendly Parks Program is a joint partnership between the U.S. Environmental Protection Agency and the National Park Service. Climate Friendly Parks from around the country are leading the way in the effort to protect our parks' natural and cultural resources and ensure their preservation for future generations; NPS image.

IV. Global Climate Change

The IPCC is a scientific intergovernmental, international body established by the World Meteorological Organization (WMO) and by the United Nations Environment Programme (UNEP). The information the IPCC provides in its reports is based on scientific evidence and reflects existing consensus viewpoints within the scientific community. The comprehensiveness of the scientific content is achieved through contributions from experts in all regions of the world and all relevant disciplines including, where appropriately documented, industry literature and traditional practices, and a two stage review process by experts and governments.

Definition of climate change: The IPCC defines climate change as a change in the state of the climate that can be identified (e.g. using statistical tests) by changes in the mean and/or the variability of its properties, and that persists for an extended period, typically decades or longer.

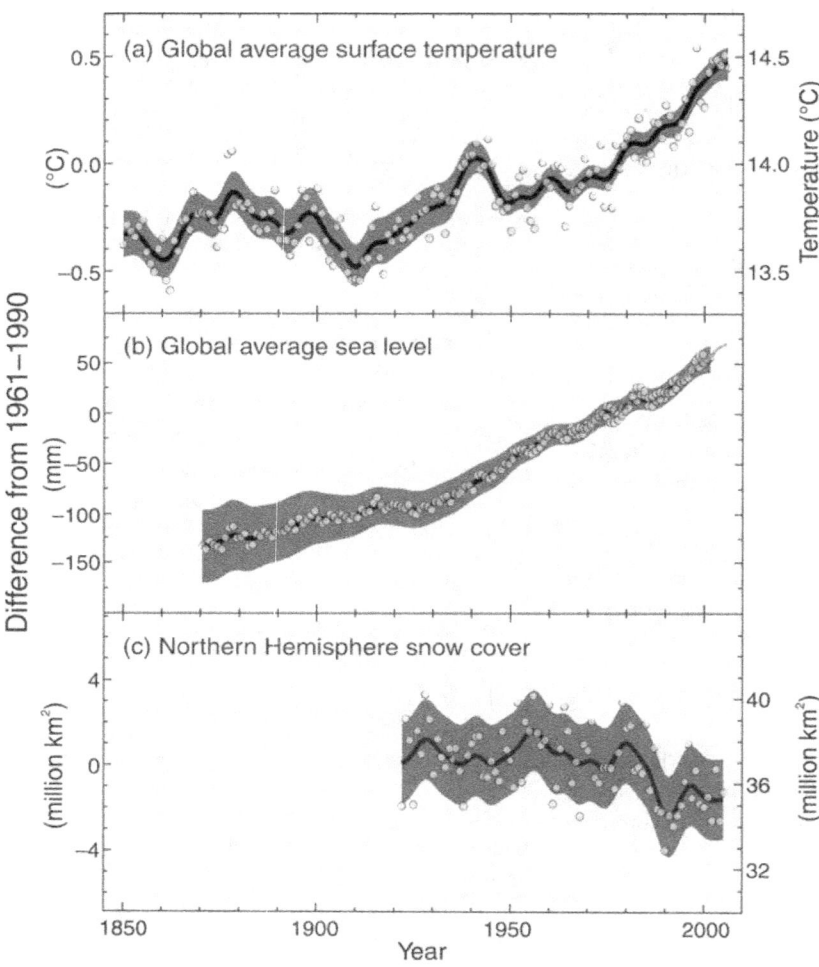

Figure 1. Observed changes in (a) global average surface temperature; (b) global average sea level from tide gauge (blue) and satellite (red) data and (c) Northern Hemisphere snow cover for March-April. All differences are relative to corresponding averages for the period 1961-1990. Smoothed curves represent decadal averaged values while circles show yearly values. The shaded areas are the uncertainty intervals estimated from a comprehensive analysis of known uncertainties (a and b) and from the time series (c) (IPCC 2007a).

A. Temperature and Greenhouse Gases

What scientists know...

- Warming of the Earth's climate system is unequivocal, as evidenced from increased air and ocean temperatures, widespread melting of snow and ice, and rising global average sea level (Figure 1).

- In the last 100 years, global average surface temperature has risen about 0.74°C over the previous 100-year period, and the rate of warming has doubled from the previous century. Eleven of the 12 warmest years in the instrumental record of global surface temperature since 1850 have occurred since 1995 (Figure 1).

- Although most regions over the globe have experienced warming, there are regional variations: land regions have warmed faster than oceans and high northern latitudes have warmed faster than the tropics. Average Arctic temperatures have increased at almost twice the global rate in the past 100 years, primarily because loss of snow and ice results in a positive feedback via increased absorption of sunlight by ocean waters (Figure 2).

- Over the past 50 years widespread changes in extreme temperatures have been observed, including a decrease in cold days and nights and an increase in the frequency of hot days, hot nights, and heat waves.

- Winter temperatures are increasing more rapidly than summer temperatures, particularly in the northern hemisphere, and

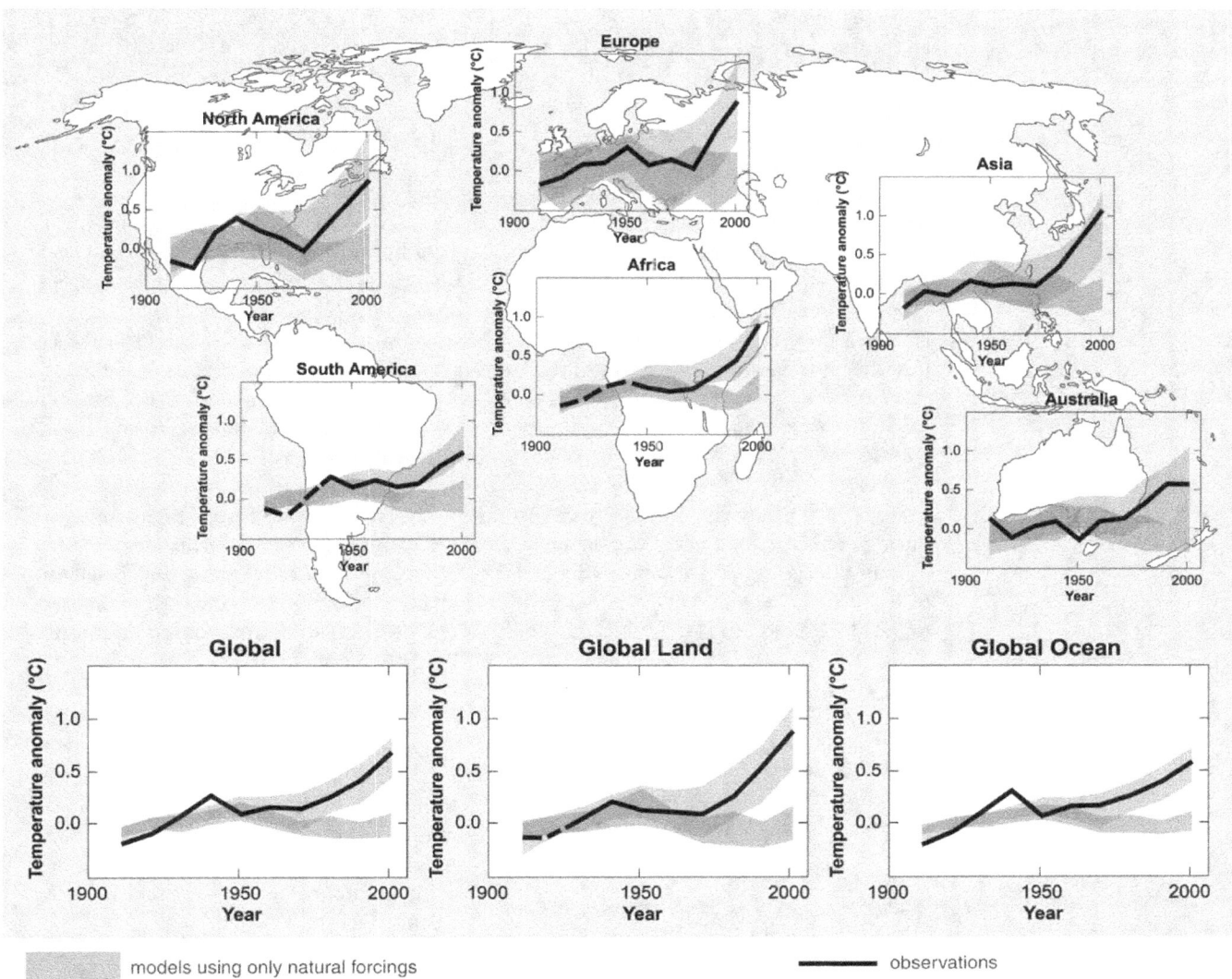

models using only natural forcings

models using both natural and anthropogenic forcings

observations

Figure 2. Comparison of observed continental- and global-scale changes in surface temperature with results simulated by climate models using either natural or both natural and anthropogenic forcings. Decadal averages of observations are shown for the period 1906-2005 (black line) plotted against the centre of the decade and relative to the corresponding average for the period 1901-1950. Lines are dashed where spatial coverage is less than 50%. Blue shaded bands show the 5 to 95% range for 19 simulations from five climate models using only the natural forcings due to solar activity and volcanoes. Red shaded bands show the 5 to 95% range for 58 simulations from 14 climate models using both natural and anthropogenic forcings (IPCC 2007a).

there has been an increase in the length of the frost-free period in mid- and high-latitude regions of both hemispheres.

- Climate change is caused by alterations in the energy balance within the atmosphere and at the Earth's surface. Factors that affect Earth's energy balance are the atmospheric concentrations of greenhouse gases and aerosols, land surface properties, and solar radiation.

- Global atmospheric concentrations of greenhouse gases have increased significantly since 1750 as the result of human activities. The principal greenhouse gases are carbon dioxide (CO_2), primarily from fossil fuel use and land-use change; methane (CH_4) and nitrous oxide (N_2O), primarily from agriculture; and halocarbons

(a group of gases containing fluorine, chlorine or bromine), principally engineered chemicals that do not occur naturally.

- Direct measurements of gases trapped in ice cores demonstrate that current CO_2 and CH_4 concentrations far exceed the natural range over the last 650,000 years and have increased markedly (35% and 148% respectively), since the beginning of the industrial era in 1750.

- Both past and future anthropogenic CO_2 emissions will continue to contribute to warming and sea level rise for more than a millennium, due to the time scales required for the removal of the gas from the atmosphere.

- Warming temperatures reduce oceanic uptake of atmospheric CO2, increasing the fraction of anthropogenic emissions remaining in the atmosphere. This positive carbon cycle feedback results in increasingly greater accumulation of atmospheric CO2 and subsequently greater warming trends than would otherwise be present in the absence of a feedback relationship.

- There is very high confidence that the global average net effect of human activities since 1750 has been one of warming.

- Scientific evidence shows that major and widespread climate changes have occurred with startling speed. For example, roughly half the north Atlantic warming during the last 20,000 years was achieved in only a decade, and it was accompanied by significant climatic changes across most of the globe (NRC 2008).

What scientists think is likely...

- Anthropogenic warming over the last three decades has likely had a discernible influence at the global scale on observed changes in many physical and biological systems.

- Average temperatures in the Northern Hemisphere during the second half of the 20th century were very likely higher than during any other 50-year period in the last 500 years and likely the highest in at least the past 1300 years.

- Most of the warming that has occurred since the mid-20th century is very likely due to increases in anthropogenic greenhouse gas concentrations. Furthermore, it is extremely likely that global changes observed in the past 50 years can only be explained with external (anthropogenic) forcings (Figure 2).

- There is much evidence and scientific consensus that greenhouse gas emissions will continue to grow under current climate change mitigation policies and development practices. For the next two decades a warming of about 0.2°C per decade is projected for a range of emissions scenarios; afterwards, temperature projections increasingly depend on specific emissions scenarios (Table 1).

- It is very likely that continued greenhouse gas emissions at or above the current rate will cause further warming and result in changes in the global climate system that will be larger than those observed during the 20th century.

- It is very likely that hot extremes, heat waves and heavy precipitation events will become more frequent. As with current trends, warming is expected to be greatest over land and at most high northern latitudes, and least over the Southern Ocean (near Antarctica) and the northern North Atlantic Ocean.

What scientists think is possible...

- Global temperatures are projected to increase in the future, and the magnitude of temperature change depends on specific emissions scenarios, and ranges from a 1.1°C to 6.4°C increase by 2100 (Table 1).

Table 1. Projected global average surface warming at the end of the 21st century, adapted from (IPCC 2007b).

Notes: a) Temperatures are assessed best estimates and likely uncertainty ranges from a hierarchy of models of varying complexity as well as observational constraints. b) Temperature changes are expressed as the difference from the period 1980-1999. To express the change relative to the period 1850-1899 add 0.5°C. c) Year 2000 constant composition is derived from Atmosphere-Ocean General Circulation Models (AOGCMs) only.

Emissions Scenario	Temperature Change (°C at 2090 – 2099 relative to 1980 – 1999)[a,b]	
	Best Estimate	Likely Range
Constant Year 2000 Concentrations[a]	0.6	0.3 – 0.9
B$_1$ Scenario	1.8	1.1 – 2.9
B$_2$ Scenario	2.4	1.4 – 3.8
A$_1$B Scenario	2.8	1.7 – 4.4
A$_2$ Scenario	3.4	2.0 – 5.4
A$_1$F$_1$ Scenario	4.0	2.4 – 6.4

Figure 3. Sea ice concentrations (the amount of ice in a given area) simulated by the GFDL CM2.1 global coupled climate model averaged over August, September and October (the months when Arctic sea ice concentrations generally are at a minimum). Three years (1885, 1985 & 2085) are shown to illustrate the model-simulated trend. A dramatic reduction of summertime sea ice is projected, with the rate of decrease being greatest during the 21st century portion. The colors range from dark blue (ice free) to white (100% sea ice covered); Image courtesy of NOAA GFDL.

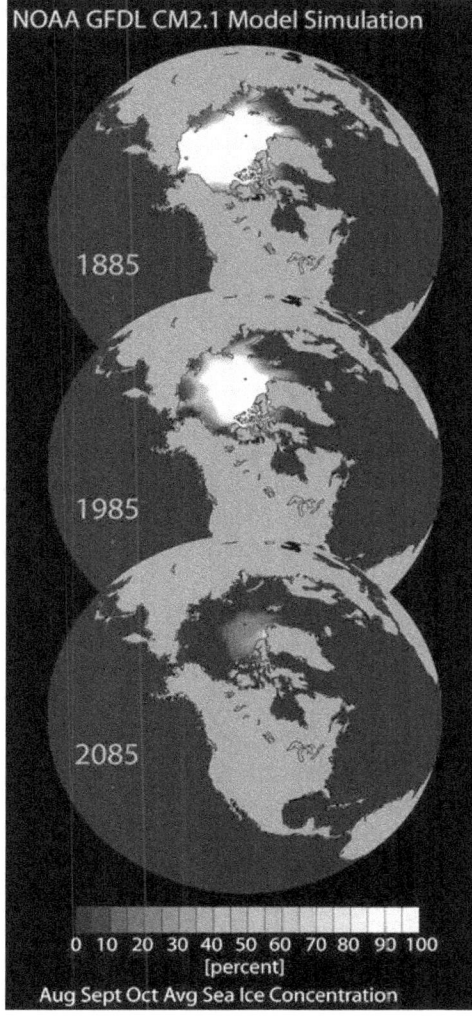

Aug Sept Oct Avg Sea Ice Concentration

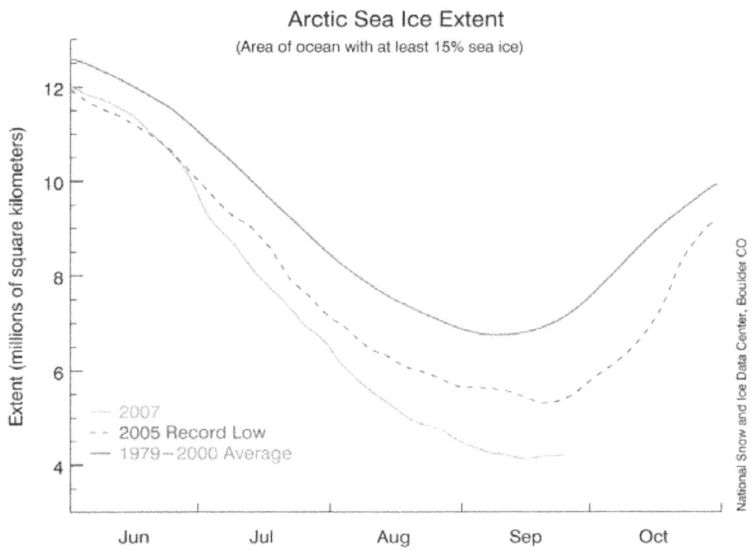

Figure 4. Arctic sea ice in September 2007 (blue line) is far below the previous low record year of 2005 (dashed line), and was 39% below where we would expect to be in an average year (solid gray line). Average September sea ice extent from 1979 to 2000 was 7.04 million square kilometers. The climatological minimum from 1979 to 2000 was 6.74 million square kilometers (NSIDC 2008).

- Anthropogenic warming could lead to changes in the global system that are abrupt and irreversible, depending on the rate and magnitude of climate change.

- Roughly 20-30% of species around the globe could become extinct if global average temperatures increase by 2 to 3°C over pre-industrial levels.

B. Water, Snow, and Ice

What scientists know...

- Many natural systems are already being affected by increased temperatures, particularly those related to snow, ice, and frozen ground. Examples are decreases in snow and ice extent, especially of mountain glaciers; enlargement and increased numbers of glacial lakes; decreased permafrost extent; increasing ground instability in permafrost regions and rock avalanches in mountain regions; and thinner sea ice and shorter freezing seasons of lake and river ice (Figure 3).

- Annual average Arctic sea ice extent has shrunk by 2.7% per decade since 1978, and the summer ice extent has decreased by 7.4% per decade. Sea ice extent during the 2007 melt season plummeted to the lowest levels since satellite measurements began in 1979, and at the end of the melt season September 2007 sea ice was 39% below the long-term (1979-2000) average (NSIDC 2008)(Figure 4).

- Global average sea level rose at an average rate of 1.8 mm per year from 1961 to 2003 and at an average rate of 3.1 mm per year from 1993 to 2003. Increases in sea level since 1993 are the result of the following contributions: thermal expansion, 57%; melting glaciers and ice caps, 28%, melting polar ice sheets, 15%.

- The CO_2 content of the oceans increased by 118 ± 19 Gt (1 Gt = 109 tons) between A.D. 1750 (the end of the pre-industrial period) and 1994 as the result of uptake of anthropogenic CO_2 emissions from the atmosphere, and continues to increase by about 2 Gt each year (Sabine et al. 2004; Hoegh-Guldberg et al. 2007). This increase in oceanic CO_2 has resulted in a 30% increase in acidity (a decrease in surface ocean pH by an average of 0.1 units), with observed and potential severe negative consequences for marine organisms and coral reef formations (Orr et al. 2005: McNeil and Matear 2007; Riebesell et al. 2009).

• Oceans are noisier due to ocean acidification reducing the ability of seawater to absorb low frequency sounds (noise from ship traffic and military activities). Low-frequency sound absorption has decreased over 10% in both the Pacific and Atlantic over the past 200 years. An assumed additional pH drop of 0.3 (due to anthropogenic CO_2 emissions) accompanied with warming will lead to sound absorption below 1 kHz being reduced by almost half of current values (Hester et. al. 2008).

• Even if greenhouse gas concentrations are stabilized at current levels thermal expansion of ocean waters (and resulting sea level rise) will continue for many centuries, due to the time required to transport heat into the deep ocean.

• Observations since 1961 show that the average global ocean temperature has increased to depths of at least 3000 meters, and that the ocean has been taking up over 80% of the heat added to the climate system.

• Hydrologic effects of climate change include increased runoff and earlier spring peak discharge in many glacier- and snow-fed rivers, and warming of lakes and rivers.

• Runoff is projected to increase by 10 to 40% by mid-century at higher latitudes and in some wet tropical areas, and to decrease by 10 to 30% over some dry regions at mid-latitudes and dry tropics. Areas in which runoff is projected to decline face a reduction in the value of the services provided by water resources.

• Precipitation increased significantly from 1900 to 2005 in eastern parts of North and South America, northern Europe, and northern and central Asia. Conversely, precipitation declined in the Sahel, the Mediterranean, southern Africa, and parts of southern Asia (Figure 5).

What scientists think is likely....

• Widespread mass losses from glaciers and reductions in snow cover are projected to accelerate throughout the 21st century, reducing water availability and changing seasonality of flow patterns.

• Model projections include contraction of snow cover area, widespread increases in depth to frost in permafrost areas, and Arctic and Antarctic sea ice shrinkage.

• The incidence of extreme high sea level has likely increased at a broad range of sites worldwide since 1975.

• Based on current model simulations it is very likely that the meridional overturning circulation (MOC) of the Atlantic Ocean will slow down during the 21st century; nevertheless regional temperatures are predicted to increase. Large-scale and persistent changes in the MOC may result in changes in marine ecosystem produc-

Figure 5. Relative changes in precipitation (in percent) for the period 2090-2099, relative to 1980-1999. Values are multi-model averages based on the SRES A₁B scenario for December to February (left) and June to August (right). White areas are where less than 66% of the models agree in the sign of the change and stippled areas are where more than 90% of the models agree in the sign of the change (IPCC 2007a).

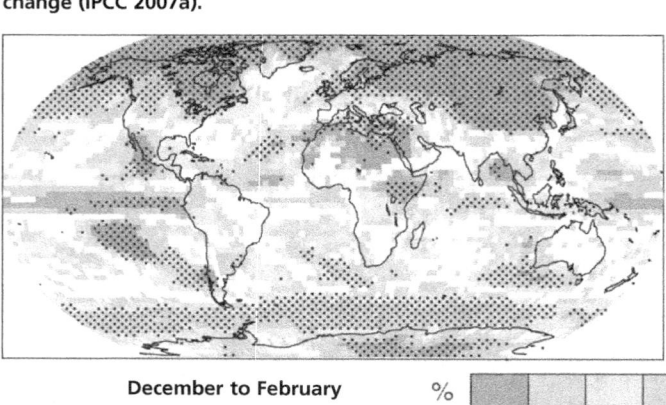

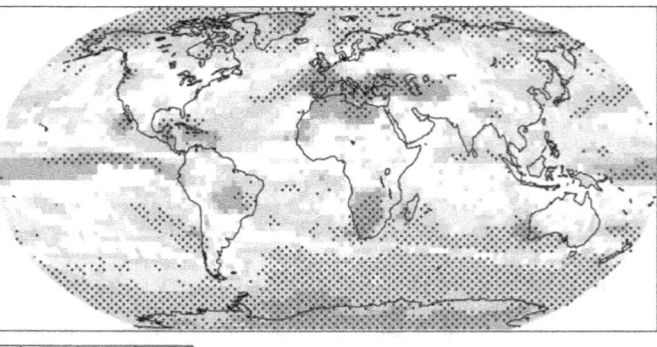

December to February   %   June to August

-20   -10   -5   5   10   20

Table 2. Projected global average sea level rise at the end of the 21st century, adapted from IPCC 2007b.

Notes: a) Temperatures are assessed best estimates and likely uncertainty ranges from a hierarchy of models of varying complexity as well as observational constraints.

Emissions Scenario	Sea level rise (m at 2090 – 2099 relative to 1980 – 1999)
	Model-based range (excluding future rapid dynamical changes in ice flow)
Constant Year 2000 Concentrations[a]	0.3 – 0.9
B$_1$ Scenario	1.1 – 2.9
B$_2$ Scenario	1.4 – 3.8
A$_1$B Scenario	1.7 – 4.4
A$_2$ Scenario	2.0 – 5.4
A$_1$F$_1$ Scenario	2.4 – 6.4

tivity, fisheries, ocean CO2 uptake, and terrestrial vegetation.

- Globally the area affected by drought has likely increased since the 1970s and the frequency of extreme precipitation events has increased over most areas.

- Future tropical cyclones (typhoons and hurricanes) are likely to become more intense, with larger peak wind speeds and increased heavy precipitation. Extra-tropical storm tracks are projected to move poleward, with consequent shifts in wind, precipitation, and temperature patterns.

- Increases in the amount of precipitation are very likely in high latitudes and decreases are likely in most subtropical land regions, continuing observed patterns (Figure 5).

- Increases in the frequency of heavy precipitation events in the coming century are very likely, resulting in potential damage to crops and property, soil erosion, surface and groundwater contamination, and increased risk of human death and injury.

What scientists think is possible...

- Arctic late-summer sea ice may disappear almost entirely by the end of the 21st century (Figure 3).

- Current global model studies project that the Antarctic ice sheet will remain too cold for widespread surface melting and gain mass due to increased snowfall. However, net loss of ice mass could occur if dynami-

cal ice discharge dominates the ice sheet mass balance.

- Model-based projections of global average sea level rise at the end of the 21st century range from 0.18 to 0.59 meters, depending on specific emissions scenarios (Table 2). These projections may actually underestimate future sea level rise because they do not include potential feedbacks or full effects of changes in ice sheet flow.

- Partial loss of ice sheets and/or the thermal expansion of seawater over very long time scales could result in meters of sea level rise, major changes in coastlines and inundation of low-lying areas, with greatest effects in river deltas and low-lying islands.

C. Vegetation and Wildlife

What scientists know...

- Temperature increases have affected Arctic and Antarctic ecosystems and predator species at high levels of the food web.

- Changes in water temperature, salinity, oxygen levels, circulation, and ice cover in marine and freshwater ecosystems have resulted in shifts in ranges and changes in algal, plankton, and fish abundance in high-latitude oceans; increases in algal and zooplankton abundance in high-latitude and high-altitude lakes; and range shifts and earlier fish migrations in rivers.

- High-latitude (cooler) ocean waters are currently acidified enough to start dissolving pteropods; open water marine snails which are one of the primary food sources of young salmon and mackerel (Fabry et al. 2008, Feely et al. 2008). In lower latitude (warmer) waters, by the end of this century Humboldt squid's metabolic rate will be reduced by 31% and activity levels by 45% due to reduced pH, leading to squid retreating at night to shallower waters to feed and replenish oxygen levels (Rosa and Seibel 2008).

- A meta-analysis of climate change effects on range boundaries in Northern Hemisphere species of birds, butterflies, and alpine herbs shows an average shift of 6.1 kilometers per decade northward (or 6.1 meters per decade upward), and a mean shift toward earlier onset of spring events (frog breeding, bird nesting, first flowering, tree budburst, and arrival of migrant butterflies and birds) of 2.3 days per decade (Parmesan and Yohe 2003).

- Poleward range shifts of individual species and expansions of warm-adapted communities have been documented on all continents and in most of the major oceans of the world (Parmesan 2006).

- Satellite observations since 1980 indicate a trend in many regions toward earlier greening of vegetation in the spring linked to longer thermal growing seasons resulting from recent warming.

- Over the past 50 years humans have changed ecosystems more rapidly and extensively than in any previous period of human history, primarily as the result of growing demands for food, fresh water, timber, fiber, and fuel. This has resulted in a substantial and largely irreversible loss of Earth's biodiversity

- Although the relationships have not been quantified, it is known that loss of intact ecosystems results in a reduction in ecosystem services (clean water, carbon sequestration, waste decomposition, crop pollination, etc.).

What scientists think is likely...

- The resilience of many ecosystems is likely to be exceeded this century by an unprecedented combination of climate change, associated disturbance (flooding, drought, wildfire, insects, ocean acidification) and other global change drivers (land use change, pollution, habitat fragmentation, invasive species, resource over-exploitation) (Figure 6).

- Exceedance of ecosystem resilience may be characterized by threshold-type responses such as extinctions, disruption of ecological interactions, and major changes in ecosystem structure and disturbance regimes.

- Net carbon uptake by terrestrial ecosystems is likely to peak before mid-century and then weaken or reverse, amplifying climate changes. By 2100 the terrestrial biosphere is likely to become a carbon source.

- Increases in global average temperature above 1.5 to 2.5°C and concurrent atmospheric CO_2 concentrations are projected to result in major changes in ecosystem structure and function, species' ecological interactions, and species' geographical ranges. Negative consequences are projected for species biodiversity and ecosystem goods and services.

- Model projections for increased atmospheric CO_2 concentration and global temperatures significantly exceed values for at least the past 420,000 years, the period during which more extant marine organisms evolved. Under expected 21st century conditions it is likely that global warming and ocean acidification will compromise carbonate accretion, resulting in less diverse reef communities and failure of some existing carbonate reef structures. Climate changes will likely exacerbate local stresses from declining water quality and overexploitation of key species (Hoegh-Guldberg et al. 2007).

- Ecosystems likely to be significantly impacted by changing climatic conditions include:

  i. Terrestrial – tundra, boreal forest, and mountain regions (sensitivity to warming); Mediterranean-type ecosystems and tropical rainforests (decreased rainfall)

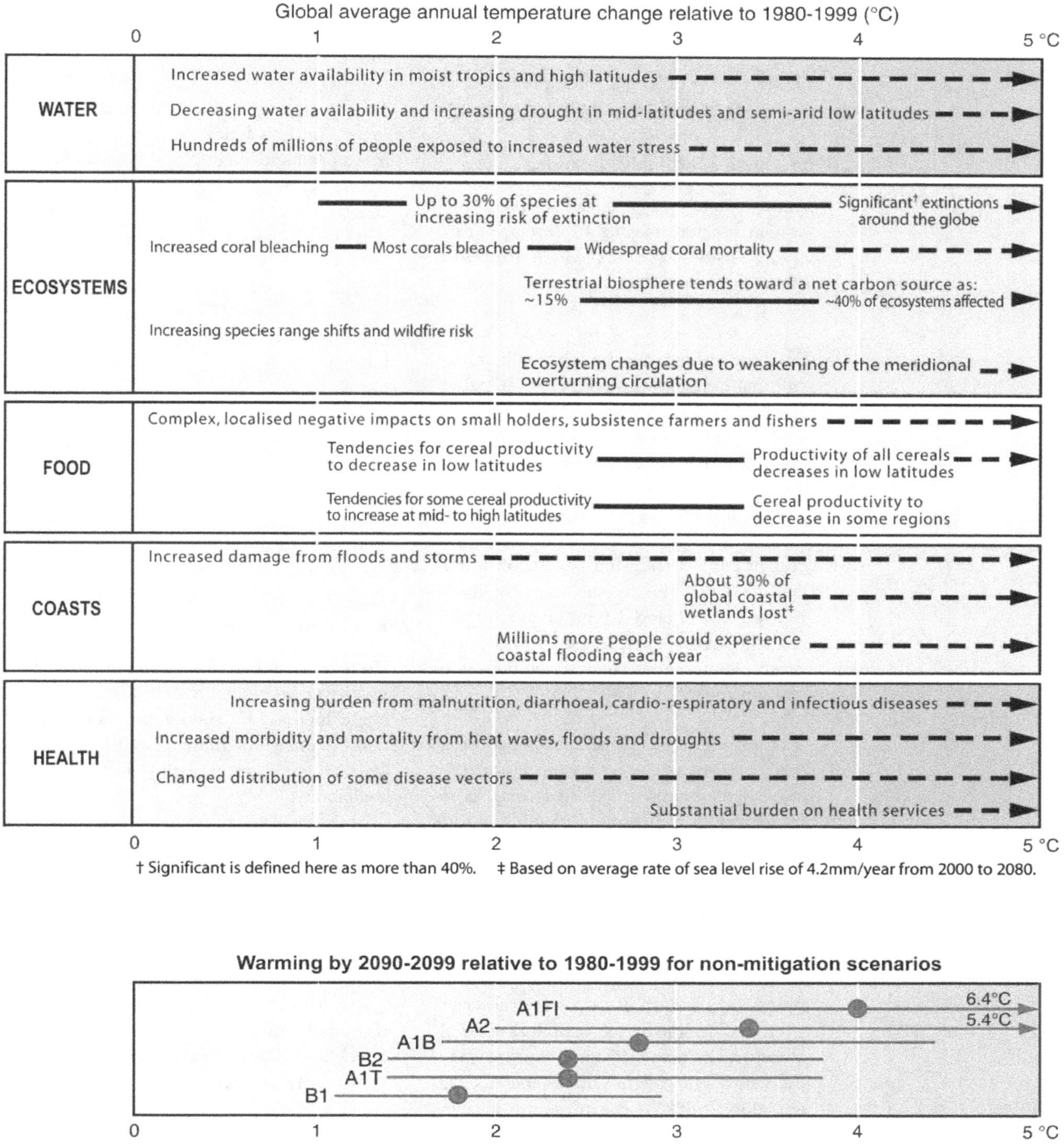

Global average annual temperature change relative to 1980-1999 (°C)

0   1   2   3   4   5 °C

WATER
- Increased water availability in moist tropics and high latitudes ➤
- Decreasing water availability and increasing drought in mid-latitudes and semi-arid low latitudes ➤
- Hundreds of millions of people exposed to increased water stress ➤

ECOSYSTEMS
- Up to 30% of species at increasing risk of extinction ——— Significant[†] extinctions around the globe ➤
- Increased coral bleaching — Most corals bleached — Widespread coral mortality ➤
- Terrestrial biosphere tends toward a net carbon source as: ~15% ——————— ~40% of ecosystems affected ➤
- Increasing species range shifts and wildfire risk
- Ecosystem changes due to weakening of the meridional overturning circulation ➤

FOOD
- Complex, localised negative impacts on small holders, subsistence farmers and fishers ➤
- Tendencies for cereal productivity to decrease in low latitudes ——— Productivity of all cereals decreases in low latitudes ➤
- Tendencies for some cereal productivity to increase at mid- to high latitudes ——— Cereal productivity to decrease in some regions

COASTS
- Increased damage from floods and storms ➤
- About 30% of global coastal wetlands lost[‡] ➤
- Millions more people could experience coastal flooding each year ➤

HEALTH
- Increasing burden from malnutrition, diarrhoeal, cardio-respiratory and infectious diseases ➤
- Increased morbidity and mortality from heat waves, floods and droughts ➤
- Changed distribution of some disease vectors ➤
- Substantial burden on health services ➤

0   1   2   3   4   5 °C

† Significant is defined here as more than 40%.   ‡ Based on average rate of sea level rise of 4.2mm/year from 2000 to 2080.

Warming by 2090-2099 relative to 1980-1999 for non-mitigation scenarios

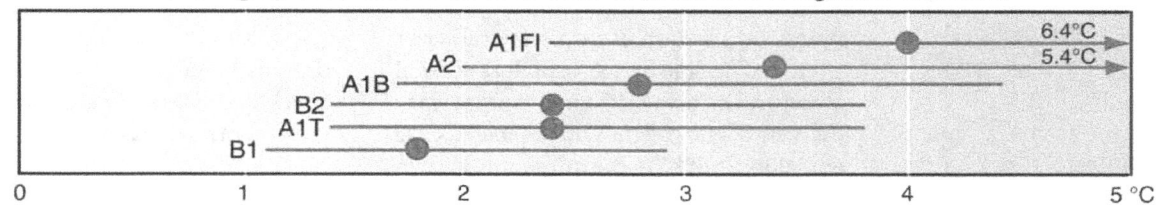

0   1   2   3   4   5 °C

Figure 6. Examples of impacts associated with projected global average surface warming. Upper panel: Illustrative examples of global impacts projected for climate changes (and sea level and atmospheric CO$_2$ where relevant) associated with different amounts of increase in global average surface temperature in the 21st century. The black lines link impacts; broken-line arrows indicate impacts continuing with increasing temperature. Entries are placed so that the left-hand side of text indicates the approximate level of warming that is associated with the onset of a given impact. Quantitative entries for water scarcity and flooding represent the additional impacts of climate change relative to the conditions projected across the range of SRES scenarios A1FI, A2, B1 and B2. Adaptation to climate change is not included in these estimations. Confidence levels for all statements are high. Lower panel: Dots and bars indicate the best estimate and likely ranges of warming assessed for the six SRES marker scenarios for 2090-2099 relative to 1980-1999 (IPCC 2007a).

ii. Coastal – mangroves and salt marshes (multiple stresses)

iii. Marine – coral reefs (multiple stresses); sea-ice biomes (sensitivity to warming)

What scientists think is possible...

- Approximately 20% to 30% of plant and animal species assessed to date are at increased risk of extinction with increases in global average temperature in excess of 1.5 to 2.5°C.

- Endemic species may be more vulnerable to climate changes, and therefore at higher risk for extinction, because they may have evolved in locations where paleo-climatic conditions have been stable.

- Although there is great uncertainty about how forests will respond to changing climate and increasing levels of atmospheric CO_2, the factors that are most typically predicted to influence forests are increased fire, increased drought, and greater vulnerability to insects and disease (Brown 2008).

- If atmospheric CO_2 levels reach 450 ppm (projected to occur by 2030–2040 at the current emissions rates), reefs may experience rapid and terminal decline worldwide from multiple climate change-related direct and indirect effects including mass bleaching, ocean acidification, damage to shallow reef communities, reduction of biodiversity, and extinctions. (Veron et al. 2009). At atmospheric CO_2 levels of 560 ppmv, calcification of tropical corals is expected to decline by 30%, and loss of coral structure in areas of high erosion may outpace coral growth. With unabated CO_2 emissions, 70% of the presently known reef locations (including cold-water corals) will be in corrosive waters by the end of this century (Riebesell, et al. 2009).

D. Disturbance

What scientists know...

- Climate change currently contributes to the global burden of disease and premature death through exposure to extreme events and changes in water and air qual-ity, food quality and quantity, ecosystems, agriculture, and economy (Parry et al. 2007).

- The most vulnerable industries, settlements, and societies are generally those in coastal and river flood plains, those whose economies are closely linked with climate-sensitive resources, and those in areas prone to extreme weather events.

- By 2080-2090 millions more people than today are projected to experience flooding due to sea level rise, especially those in the low-lying megadeltas of Asia and Africa and on small islands.

- Climate change affects the function and operation of existing water infrastructure and water management practices, aggravating the impacts of population growth, changing economic activity, land-use change, and urbanization.

What scientists think is likely...

- Up to 20% of the world's population will live in areas where river flood potential could increase by 2080-2090, with major consequences for human health, physical infrastructure, water quality, and resource availability.

- The health status of millions of people is projected to be affected by climate change, through increases in malnutrition; increased deaths, disease, and injury due to extreme weather events; increased burden of diarrheal diseases; increased cardio-respiratory disease due to higher concentrations of ground-level ozone in urban areas; and altered spatial distribution of vector-borne diseases.

- Risk of hunger is projected to increase at lower latitudes, especially in seasonally dry and tropical regions.

What scientists think is possible...

- Although many diseases are projected to increase in scope and incidence as the result of climate changes, lack of appropriate longitudinal data on climate change-related health impacts precludes definitive assessment.

V. References

Abatzoglou, J. T. and K. T. Redmond. 2007. Asymmetry between trends in spring and autumn temperature and circulation regimes over western North America. Geophysical Research Letters 34:1-5.

Amelung, B., S. Nicholls, and D. Viner. 2007. Implications of global climate change for tourism flows and seasonality. Journal of Travel Research 45:285.

Barnett, T., R. Malone, W. Pennell, D. Stammer, B. Semtner, and W. Washington. 2004. The effects of climate change on water resources in the west: Introduction and overview. Climatic Change 62:1-11.

Barnett, T. P., D. W. Pierce, H. G. Hidalgo, C. Bonfils, B. D. Santer, T. Das, G. Bala, A. W. Wood, T. Nozawa, and A. A. Mirin. 2008. Human-induced changes in the hydrology of the western United States. Science 319:1080.

Baron, J. S., M. D. Hartman, L. E. Band, and R. B. Lammers. 2000. Sensitivity of a high elevation Rocky Mountain watershed to altered climate and CO_2. Water Resources Research 36:89–99.

Beever, E. A., P. F. Brussard, and J. Berger. 2003. Patterns of apparent extirpation among isolated population of pikas (Ochotona princeps) in the Great Basin. Journal of Mammalogy 84:37-54.

Brown, R. 2008. The implications of climate change for conservation, restoration, and management of National Forest lands. National Forest Restoration Collaborative.

Burkett, V. R., D. A. Wilcox, R. Stottlemyer, W. Barrow, D. Fagre, J. Baron, J. Price, J. L. Nielsen, C. D. Allen, D. L. Peterson, G. Ruggerone, and T. Doyle. 2005. Nonlinear dynamics in ecosystem response to climatic change: Case studies and policy implications. Ecological Complexity 2:357-394.

Burns, C. E., K. M. Johnston, and O. J. Schmitz. 2003. Global climate change and mammalian species diversity in U.S. national parks. Proceedings of the National Academy of Sciences 100:11474-11477.

Carroll, A. L. 2006. Impacts of climate change on range expansion by the mountain pine beetle. Mountain Pine Beetle Initiative Working Paper 2006-14.

CIRMOUNT. 2006. Mapping new terrain: Climate change and America's west. Report of the Consortium for Integrated Climate Research in Western Mountains (CIRMOUNT). Pacific Southwest Research Station, Forest Service, U.S. Department of Agriculture, Albany, CA.

Clow, D. W., L. Schrott, R. Webb, D. H. Campbell, A. Torizzo, and M. Dornblaser. 2003. Ground water occurrence and contributions to streamflow in an alpine catchment, Colorado Front Range. Ground Water 41:937-950.

Confalonieri, U., B. Menne, R. Akhtar, K. L. Ebi, M. Hauengue, R. S. Kovats, B. Revich, and A. Woodward. 2007. Human health. Climate change 2007: Impacts, adaptation and vulnerability. Contribution of Working Group II to the Fourth Assessment Report of the Intergovernmental Panel on Climate Change, M.L. Parry, O.F. Canziani, J.P. Palutikof, P.J. van der Linden and C.E. Hanson, Eds., Cambridge University Press, Cambridge, UK, 391-431.

Cooney, S. J., A. P. Covich, P. M. Lukacs, A. L. Harig, and K. D. Fausch. 2005. Modeling global warming scenarios in greenback cutthroat trout (Oncorhynchus clarki stomias) streams: implications for species recovery. Western North American Naturalist 65:371-381.

Crozier, L. 2003. Winter warming facilitates range expansion: Cold tolerance of the butterfly Atalopedes campestris. Oecologia 135:648-656.

Crozier, L. 2004. Warmer winters drive butterfly range expansion by increasing survivorship. Ecology 85:231-241.

Dale, V. H., L. A. Joyce, S. McNulty, R. P. Neilson, M. P. Ayres, M. D. Flannigan, P. J. Hanson, L. C. Irland, A. E. Lugo, and C. J. Peterson. 2001. Climate Change and forest disturbances. BioScience 51:723-734.

Dettinger, M. D., D. R. Cayan, M. K. Meyer, and A. E. Jeton. 2004. Simulated hydrologic responses to climate variations and change in the Merced, Carson, and American River basins, Sierra Nevada, California, 1900–2099. Climatic Change 62:283-317.

Diffenbaugh, N. S., J. S. Pal, R. J. Trapp, and F. Giorgi. 2005. Fine-scale processes regulate the response of extreme events to global climate change. Proceedings of the National Academy of Sciences 102:15774-15778.

Epstein, P. R. 2001. Climate change and emerging infectious diseases. Microbes and Infection 3:747-754.

Fabry, V.J, B.A. Seibel, R.A. Feely, and J.C. Orr. 2008. Impacts of ocean acidification on marine fauna and ecosystem processes. ICES Journal of Marine Science 65: 414-432.

Fagre, D. B. and D. L. Peterson. 2000. Ecosystem dynamics and disturbance in mountain wildernesses: Assessing vulnerability of natural resources to change. In Wilderness Science in a Time of Change, Vol. 3: Wilderness as a Place for Scientific Inquiry, S. F. McCool, Cole, D. N., Borrie, W. T., and O'Loughlin, J., editor. Rocky Mountain Research Station, USDA Forest Service, Ogden, UT. Pages 74-81

Fagre, D. B., D. L. Peterson, and A. E. Hessl. 2003. Taking the pulse of mountains: Ecosystem responses to climatic variability. Climatic Change 59:263-282.

Feely, R.A., C.L. Sabine, J. M. Hernandez-Ayon, D. Lanson and B. Hales. 2008. Evidence for upwelling of corrosive "acidified" water onto the continental shelf. Science 320(5882): 1490-1492.

Fenn, M. E., J. S. Baron, E. B. Allen, H. M. Rueth, K. R. Nydick, L. Geiser, W. D. Bowman, J. O. Sickman, T. Meixner, and D. W. Johnson. 2003. Ecological effects of nitrogen deposition in the western United States. BioScience 53:404-420.

Field, C. B., L.D. Mortsch, M. Brklacich, D.L. Forbes, P. Kovacs, J.A. Patz, S.W. Running, and M.J. Scott. 2007. North America. Climate change 2007: Impacts, adaptation and vulnerability. Contribution of Working Group II to the Fourth Assessment Report of the Intergovernmental Panel on Climate Change, M.L. Parry, O.F. Canziani, J.P. Palutikof, P.J. van der Linden and C.E. Hanson, Eds., Cambridge University Press, Cambridge, UK, 617-652.

Gonzalez, P., R. P. Neilson, K. S. McKelvey, J. M. Lenihan, and R. J. Drapek. 2007. Potential impacts of climate change on habitat and conservation priority areas for Lynx canadensis (Canada Lynx). The Nature Conservancy, Arlington, VA.

Hall, M. H. P. and D. B. Fagre. 2003. Modeled climate-induced glacier change in Glacier National Park, 1850–2100. BioScience 53:131-140.

Hamlet, A. F. and D. P. Lettenmaier. 2007. Effects of 20th century warming and climate variability on flood risk in the western US. Water Resources Research 43:6427.

Hamlet, A. F., P. W. Mote, M. P. Clark, and D. P. Lettenmaier. 2007. 20th century trends in runoff, evapotranspiration, and soil moisture in the western US. Journal of Climate 20:1468-1486.

Hesseln, H., J. B. Loomis, and A. González-Cabán. 2004. Comparing the economic effects of fire on hiking demand in Montana and Colorado. Journal of Forest Economics 10:21-35.

Hester, K.C., E.T. Peltzer, W.J. Kirkwood and P.G.Brewer. 2008. Unanticipated consequences of ocean acidification: A noisier ocean at lower pH. Geophysical Research Letters 35: L19601.

Heyerdahl, E. K., D. McKenzie, L. D. Daniels, A. E. Hessl, J. S. Littell, and N. J. Mantua. 2008. Climate drivers of regionally synchronous fires in the inland Northwest (1651-1900). International Journal of Wildland Fire 17:40.

Hoegh-Guldberg, O., P. J. Mumby, A. J. Hooten, R. S. Steneck, P. Greenfield, E. Gomez, C. D. Harvell, P. F. Sale, A. J. Edwards, K. Caldeira, N. Knowlton, C. M. Eakin, R. Iglesias-Prieto, N. Muthiga, R. H. Bradbury, A. Dubi and M. E. Hatziolos. 2007. Coral Reefs Under Rapid Climate Change and Ocean Acidification. Science 318: 1737-1742.

Inouye, D. W., B. Barr, K. B. Armitage, and B. D. Inouye. 2000. Climate change is affecting altitudinal migrants and hibernating species. Proceedings of the National Academy of Sciences 97:1630.

IPCC. 2007a. Climate Change 2007: Synthesis Report. Contribution of Working Groups I, II, and III to the Fourth Assessment Report of the Intergovernmental Panel on Climate Change. [Core Writing Team, Pachauri, R.K and Reisinger, A. (eds.)]. IPCC, Geneva, Switzerland, 104 pp.

IPCC. 2007b. Climate Change 2007: The Physical Science Basis. Contribution of Working Group I to the Fourth Assessment Report of the Intergovernmental Panel on Climate Change [Solomon, S., D. Qin, M. Manning, Z. Chen, M. Marquis, K.B. Averyt, M. Tignor and H.L. Miller (eds.)]. Cambridge University Press, Cambridge, United Kingdom and New York, NY, USA, 996 pp.

ISAB. 2007. Climate Change Impacts on Columbia River Basin fish and wildlife. Independent Scientific Advisory Board, Northwest Power and Conservation Council, Portland, OR.

Kharin, V. V., F. W. Zwiers, X. Zhang, and G. C. Hegerl. 2007. Changes in temperature and precipitation extremes in the IPCC ensemble of global coupled model simulations. Journal of Climate 20:1419-1444.

Knowles, N. and D. R. Cayan. 2004. Elevational dependence of projected hydrologic changes in the San Francisco estuary and watershed. Climatic Change 62:319-336.

Knowles, N., M. D. Dettinger, and D. R. Cayan. 2006. Trends in snowfall versus rainfall in the western United States. Journal of Climate 19:4545-4959.

Konrad, C. P. and D. B. Booth. 2005. Hydrologic changes in urban streams and their ecological significance. American Fisheries Society Symposium 47:157-177.

Lenihan, J. M., D. Bachelet, R. P. Neilson, and R. Drapek. 2008. Response of vegetation distribution, ecosystem productivity, and fire to climate change scenarios for California. Climatic Change 87:215-230.

Lenihan, J. M., R. Drapek, D. Bachelet, and R. P. Neilson. 2003. Climate change effects on vegetation distribution, carbon, and fire in California. Ecological Applications 13:1667-1681.

Logan, J. A. and J. A. Powell. 2001. Ghost forest, global warming, and the mountain pine beetle (Coleoptera: Scolytidae). American Entomologist 47:160-173.

Loomis, J., A. Gonzalez-Caban, and J. Englin. 2001. Testing for differential effects of forest fires on hiking and mountain biking demand and benefits. Journal of Agricultural and Resource Economics 26:508-522.

Maurer, E. P. and P. B. Duffy. 2005. Uncertainty in projections of streamflow changes due to climate change in California. Geophysical Research Letters 32:L03704.

McCarty, J. P. 2001. Ecological consequences of recent climate change. Conservation Biology 15:320-331.

McNeil, B. I. and R. J. Matear. 2007. Climate change feedbacks on future oceanic acidification. Tellus 59B: 191–198.

Millar, C. I., R. D. Westfall, D. L. Delany, J. C. King, and L. J. Graumlich. 2004. Response of subalpine conifers in the Sierra Nevada, California, USA, to 20th-century warming and decadal climate variability. Arctic, Antarctic, and Alpine Research 36:181-200.

Miller, J. D., H. D. Safford, M. Crimmins, and E. A. Thode. 2008. Quantitative evidence for increasing forest fire severity in the Sierra Nevada and southern Cascade Mountains, California and Nevada, USA. Ecosystems DOI: 10.1007/s10021-008-9201-9.

Morgan, P., E. K. Heyerdahl, and C. E. Gibson. 2008. Multi-season climate synchronized forest fires throughout the 20th century, northern Rockies, USA. Ecology 89:717-728.

Moritz, C., J. L. Patton, C. J. Conroy, J. L. Parra, G. C. White, and S. R. Beissinger. 2008. Impact of a century of climate change on small-mammal communities in Yosemite National Park, USA. Science 322:261.

Mote, P., A. Hamlet, and E. Salathe. 2008a. Has spring snowpack declined in the Washington Cascades? Hydrology and Earth System Sciences 12:193.

Mote, P., E. Salathé, V. Dulière, and E. Jump. 2008b. Scenarios of future climate for the Pacific Northwest. Climate Impacts Group, University of Washington, Seattle, WA.

Mote, P. W., A. F. Hamlet, M. P. Clark, and D. P. Lettenmaier. 2005. Declining mountain snowpack in western North America. American Meteorological Society:39-49.

NRC. 2008. Ecological impacts of climate change. The National Academies Press, Washington, D.C.

NSIDC. 2008. National Snow and Ice Data Center.

Orr, J. C., V. J. Fabry, O. Aumont, L. Bopp, S. C. Doney, R. A. Feely, A. Gnanadesikan, N. Gruber, A. Ishida and F. Joos. 2005. Anthropogenic ocean acidification over the twenty-first century and its impact on calcifying organisms. Nature 437(29): 681-686.

Pacala, S. W., G. C. Hurtt, D. Baker, P. Peylin, R. A. Houghton, R. A. Birdsey, L. Heath, E. T. Sundquist, R. F. Stallard, and P. Ciais. 2001. Consistent land-and atmosphere-based US carbon sink estimates. Science 292:2316-2320.

Parmesan, C. 2006. Ecological and evolutionary responses to recent climate change. Annual Review of Ecology, Evolution and Systematics 37:637-669.

Parmesan, C. and G. Yohe. 2003. A globally coherent fingerprint of climate change impacts across natural systems. Nature 421:37-42.

Parry, M. L., O. F. Canziani, J. P. Palutikof, and Co-authors 2007: Technical Summary. Climate Change 2007: Impacts, Adaptation and Vulnerability. Contribution of Working Group II to the Fourth Assessment Report of the Intergovernmental Panel on Climate Change, M.L. Parry, O.F. Canziani, J.P. Palutikof, P.J. van der Linden and C.E. Hanson, Eds., Cambridge University Press, Cambridge, UK, 23-78.

Patz, J. A., M. A. McGeehin, S. M. Bernard, K. L. Ebi, P. R. Epstein, A. Grambsch, D. J. Gubler, P. Reiter, I. Romieu, and J. B. Rose. 2000. The potential health impacts of climate variability and change for the United States: Executive summary of the report of the health sector of the US National Assessment. Environmental Health Perspectives 108:367-376.

Ray, A. J., J. J. Barsugli, and K. B. Averyt. 2008. Climate change in Colorado - A synthesis to support water resources management and adaptation. University of Colorado at Boulder.

Richardson, R. B. and J. B. Loomis. 2004. Adaptive recreation planning and climate change: a contingent visitation approach. Ecological Economics 50:83-99.

Riebesell, U., A. Kortzinger and A. Oschlies. 2009. Sensitivities of marine carbon fluxes to ocean change. Proceedings of the National Academy of Sciences 106(49): 20602–20609.

Root, T. L., J. Price, K. R. Hall, S. H. Schneider, C. Rosenzweig, and J. A. Pounds. 2003. Fingerprints of global warming on wild animals and plants. Nature 421:57-60.

Rosa, R. and B.A. Seibel. 2008. Synergistic effects of climate-related variables suggest future physiological impairment in a top oceanic predator. PNAS 105(52): 20776-20780.

Ryan, M. G., S.R. Archer, R. Birdsey, C. Dahm, L. Heath, J. Hicke, D. Hollinger, T. Huxman, G. Okin, R. Oren, J. Randerson, W. Schlesinger. 2008. Land resources. In The effects of climate change on agriculture, land resources, water resources, and biodiversity in the United States. A Report by the U.S. Climate Change Science Program and the Subcommittee on Global Change Research. U.S. Department of Agriculture, Washington, DC., USA.

Sabine, C. L., R. A. Feely, N. Gruber, R. M. Key, K. Lee, J. L. Bullister, R. Wanninkhof, C. S. Wong, D. W. R. Wallace, B. Tilbrook, F. J. Millero, T.-H. Peng, A. Kozyr, T. Ono and A. F. Rios. 2004. The Oceanic Sink for Anthropogenic CO2. 2004 305: 367-371.

Scavia, D., J. C. Field, D. F. Boesch, R. W. Buddemeier, V. Burkett, D. R. Cayan, M. Fogarty, M. A. Harwell, R. W. Howarth, and C. Mason. 2002. Climate change impacts on US coastal and marine ecosystems. Estuaries and Coasts 25:149-164.

Scott, D., B. Jones, and J. Konopek. 2007. Implications of climate and environmental change for nature-based tourism in the Canadian Rocky Mountains: A case study of Waterton Lakes National Park. Tourism Management 28:570-579.

Sekercioglu, C. H., S. H. Schneider, J. P. Fay, and S. R. Loarie. 2007. Climate Change, elevational range shifts, and bird extinctions. Conservation Biology:1-11.

Service, R. F. 2004. As the west goes dry. Science 303:1124-1127.

Veron, J. E. N., O. Hoegh-Guldberg, T. M. Lenton, J. M. Lough, D. O. Obura, P. Pearce-Kelly, C. R. C. Sheppard, M. Spalding, M. G. Stafford-Smith and A. D. Rogers. 2009. The coral reef crisis: The critical importance of <350 ppm CO_2. Marine Pollution Bulletin 58: 1428–1436.

Walther, G. R., E. Post, P. Convey, A. Menzel, C. Parmesan, T. J. C. Beebee, J. M. Fromentin, O. Hoegh-Guldberg, and F. Bairlein. 2002. Ecological responses to recent climate change. Nature 416:389-395.

Westerling, A. L., H. G. Hidalgo, D. R. Cayan, and T. W. Swetnam. 2006. Warming and earlier spring increase western U.S. forest wildfire activity. Science 313:940-943.

Whitlock, C., S. L. Shafer, and J. Marlon. 2003. The role of climate and vegetation change in shaping past and future fire regimes in the northwestern US and the implications for ecosystem management. Forest Ecology and Management 178:5-21.

NPS D-2046, December 2009

www.ingramcontent.com/pod-product-compliance
Lightning Source LLC
Chambersburg PA
CBHW080934290526
45795CB00007BA/2750